WORDSWORTH

WILLIAM WORDSWORTH

(Reproduced by kind permission of the owner, Mrs Rawnsley)

WORDSWORTH

by PETER BURRA

Great Lives

DUCKWORTH

3 HENRIETTA STREET
LONDON   W.C.2

First published . . 1936
Reprinted 1950

a. 1

Printed in Great Britain by
Jas. Truscott & Son Ltd., London & Tonbridge

CONTENTS

CONTENTS

ACKNOWLEDGEMENTS.

Quotations from the 1805 Text of *The Prelude* are made by kind permission of Professor E. de Selincourt and the Oxford University Press.

The portrait on the dustcover is by Henry Edridge, A.R.A. (1805), and appears by kind permission of its owner, Mrs. Rawnsley.

CHRONOLOGY

1770. April 7. William Wordsworth born at Cockermouth.

1771. Dec. 25. Dorothy born.

1772. John born.

1774. Christopher born.

1778. Death of mother. To school at Hawkshead.

1783. Death of father.

1784. The *School Exercise* written.

1787. To St. John's College, Cambridge.

1788. First summer vacation spent at Hawkshead. The " dedication."

1790. Tour on the Continent with Robert Jones.

1791. Feb. In London.

Nov. To Orleans. Meets Annette and Beaupuy.

1792. In Blois and Orleans.

Dec. (?) Return to England. Birth of Annette's child.

1793. Feb. 1. France declares war on England.

Descriptive Sketches and *An Evening Walk* published.

Summer. Journey across England. First visit to Tintern.

Oct. Probably in France.

1794. In the North of England.

1795. Jan. Death of Raisley Calvert.
Sept. Settles with Dorothy at Racedown.

1797. Visits of Mary Hutchinson and Coleridge.
July.   They move to Alfoxden.
Dec.   Short visit to London.

1798. June 26.   They leave Alfoxden.
July 13.   *Tintern Abbey* written.
Sept.   They leave for Hamburg.   *Lyrical Ballads* published.
Oct.   To Goslar.

1799. April.   Return to England.   At Sockburn.
Dec. 20.   William and Dorothy come to Dove Cottage, Grasmere.

1802. Aug.   With Annette and Caroline in Calais.
Oct. 4.   William marries Mary Hutchinson

1803. June 18.   Birth of their son John.
Autumn.   Tour in Scotland.   Meets Scott.

1804. Coleridge leaves for Malta.
Aug. 16.   Birth of Dora.

1805. Feb. 5.   Brother John drowned.
Autumn.   Visit from Scott.

1806. June 16.   Thomas born.
Oct.   They go to Coleorton.

1807. Jan.   Reading of *The Prelude* to Coleridge.
May.   *Poems in Two Volumes*, published.

1808. June.   They move to Allan Bank.
Sept. 6.   Birth of Catherine.

1809. May.   " Convention of Cintra " Tract published.

1810. May 12.   William born.
Oct.   Estrangement from Coleridge.

1811. Spring.   Removal to Rectory.

1812. June 4.   Death of Catherine.
Dec. 1.   Death of Thomas.

1813. Spring. Removal to Rydal Mount.
March. Wordsworth appointed Distributor of Stamps for Westmorland.

1814. Aug. *The Excursion* published.

1815. May. *White Doe of Rylstone* published.

1818. Active politics on behalf of Lord Lonsdale. *Lines Composed Upon an Evening of Extraordinary Splendour.*

1819. *Peter Bell* and *The Waggoner* published.

1820. July – Nov. Continental tour.

1823. Tour of Holland and Belgium.

1828. Rhine tour with Dora and Coleridge.

1829. Dorothy taken ill.

1833. Tour in the Isle of Man and Scotland.

1834. Deaths of Coleridge and Lamb.

1835. *Yarrow Revisited*, etc., published. *Extempore Effusion* written.

1837. Last Continental tour.

1839. D.C.L. at Oxford.

1841. Visit to West Country. Dora's marriage.

1843. Poet Laureate.

1847. Death of Dora.

1850. April 23. Death of Wordsworth.

1855. Death of Dorothy.

1859. Death of Mary.

To
W. M. HOWITT

CHAPTER I

1770–1788

Living and remembering – early days – " endless imitation " – school at Hawkshead – " glad animal movements " – the beginning of Poetry – Cambridge – the expanding vision – first summer vacation – " a dedicated Spirit."

" Archimedes said that he could move the world if he had a point whereon to rest his machine. Who has not felt the same aspirations as regards the world of his own mind ? " Searching for the fixed point upon which his poetry might rest and turn over the invisible hemisphere of that mind-world into the light, Wordsworth allowed himself to imagine an existence before birth, from which, " trailing clouds of glory," the human child came. Yet the earth to which he was born was so filled with glories of her own that, long before the mind learnt to recognise differences, the power vanished of saying which were the natural glories, which the trailed clouds.

" Each man," wrote Wordsworth, " is a memory to himself " ; and in the pursuit of that memory, the serious recollection of those " points . . . within our Souls, where all stand single," lies the only chance vouchsafed us of seeing all round the globe of life. But memory is piled upon memory, and in Time's confusion one is lost in another, so that even of our unimagined history in " the world which is the very world " nothing remains certain except that a lost child was the father of this man.

Before he had completed half of his long life Wordsworth wrote the great autobiographical poem on the Growth of a Poet's Mind, because such remembrances as an ordered self-examination might bring out of things past were the sole evidences accessible to him in his aspiration to penetrate the mysteries of things. He employed a marvellously apt image to describe the search:

As one who hangs down-bending from the side
Of a slow-moving Boat, upon the breast
Of a still water, solacing himself
With such discoveries as his eye can make,
Beneath him, in the bottom of the deeps,
Sees many beauteous sights, weeds, fishes, flowers,
Grots, pebbles, roots of trees, and fancies more ;
Yet often is perplex'd, and cannot part
The shadow from the substance, rocks and sky,
Mountains and clouds, from that which is indeed
The region, and the things which there abide
In their true dwelling ; now is cross'd by gleam
Of his own image, by a sunbeam now,
And motions that are sent he knows not whence,
Impediments that make his task more sweet ;
—Such pleasant office have we long pursued
Incumbent o'er the surface of past time.

One is reminded of Proust both in the method and in many of the recollections. Wordsworth recognised that in the long existence of common daily life certain " spots of time " stand out,

Which with distinct pre-eminence retain
A vivifying Virtue ;

sudden perceptions of beauty – crowds of dancing daffodils by the lakeside, lovely chance words spoken by passing strangers, moments of childish fear or guilt. After a time he learnt by experience to value them still more deeply at the time of sensation, from the knowledge that they possessed the power to re-create themselves at will in future years. There was a " spiritual presence " in all past or absent things. Out of this recollection of the emotion in tranquillity his poems were made. His poetry was a planned attempt to link the different parts of his life together, to bind his days each to each with natural piety, so that the present man might achieve the great art of knowing himself.

The difficulty for Wordsworth – and how much more is it so for the biographer – was that the present man always threw something of his shadow back over all those past moments. The gesture of impatience at Tintern – " I cannot paint what then I was " – is developed in *The Prelude* into :

> I cannot say what portion is in truth
> The naked recollection of that time,
> And what may rather have been call'd to life
> By after-meditation ;

and when he looked right back to childhood, he seemed

> Two consciousnesses, conscious of myself
> And of some other Being.

As man and a poet he believed that his first labour should be to identify those two beings so far as to recognise the growth of the one into the other, and yet not to confuse them. Stripping away so far as was possible the impressions laid over the past by philosophic years, he approaches the half-opened hiding-places of his power :

Oh ! mystery of Man, from what a depth
Proceed thy honours ! I am lost, but see
In simple childhood something of the base
On which thy greatness stands.

He fell into the sleep and forgetting of life
on April 7th, 1770, the second child of his
parents, in a plain but stately house in Cockermouth which his father, John Wordsworth, an
attorney, occupied as law-agent to Sir James
Lowther, later Earl of Lonsdale. The earliest
picture in his memories was the line of white road
which he saw each day from the windows, dis-
appearing far away over the hill. It drew his
thoughts already out of their first tiny limits, " a
guide into eternity " and " to things unknown
and without bound." In that symbol was contained the whole future action of the outer world
upon his mind, at once its imaginative summons
to pass beyond every " wall or gulf of mystery "
and its call upon his passion to share the life of
the " Wanderers of the Earth." A garden led
down from the back of the house to a terrace,
where there were butterflies and birds, destined
to live with him long beyond their present hour ;
and beneath the terrace, Derwent,

the fairest of all Rivers, lov'd
To blend his murmurs with my Nurse's song,
And from his alder shades and rocky falls,
And from his fords and shallows, sent a voice
That flow'd along my dreams.

All through his life the waters of rivers were to
mingle with his poetry, and in almost his last
piece he tells how their " unremitting voices "

> mix with sleep
> To regulate the motion of our dreams
> For kindly issues.

Soon, when the bounds were extending, he " many a time "

> Made one long bathing of a summer's day,
> Bask'd in the sun, and plung'd and bask'd again
> Alternate all a summer's day, or cours'd
> Over the sandy fields, leaping through groves
> Of yellow grunsel, or when crag and hill,
> The woods and distant Skiddaw's lofty height,
> Were bronz'd with a deep radiance, stood alone
> Beneath the sky, as if I had been born
> On Indian Plains, and from my Mother's hut
> Had run abroad in wantonness, to sport,
> A naked Savage, in the thunder shower.

For a savage he was born, as much an animal as a man. He came to glory in the memory of it, as part of a divine inheritance. He was, he tells us, " of a stiff, moody, and violent temper." He once stuck his whip through a family portrait, after first daring his elder brother Richard to do it ; and once in a frenzy he went up to the attic of his grandfather Cookson's house in Penrith with the intention of killing himself with one of the foils which were kept there. The heroic mastery of himself and of his griefs which he achieved in later years can only be appreciated in the light of this innate passion.

There were many early influences at work for his gentleness, and the chief of these was his mother, who once said that " the only one of her five children about whose future she was anxious was William ; and he would be remarkable either for good or for evil." By an odd trick of memory, the only pictures he could recall of her – except for the vague consciousness of

> that first time
> In which, a Babe, by intercourse of touch,
> I held mute dialogues with my Mother's heart –

were associated with visits to the church in which he was baptised and brought up. It seemed to him who honoured her " in perfect love " a rare advantage in those times that, rejecting the eccentric fashions of modernism in education, she had trusted patiently in nature and in her children as they had been made. She died, aged thirty, when he was hardly eight years old.

His sister Dorothy, twenty months his junior, was born in 1771 on Christmas Day. Their companionship, rich in the sharing of gifts, was to last all their lives. Her love of William, she once said, was " the building up of my being, the light of my path." And he thanked her for the " eyes and ears " which she gave him, fixing his imagination on the details of the world. He recalled in after years how he, " a very hunter," would rush upon a butterfly,

> But she, God love her ! feared to brush
> The dust from off its wings ;

and how, when the sparrow built in the hedges on the terrace wall and they visited the nest together,

> She looked at it and seemed to fear it ;
> Dreading, tho' wishing, to be near it :
> Such heart was in her, being then
> A little Prattler among men :

and how when at Whitehaven she first heard and saw the sea she burst into tears.

When he was an old man dictating the notes on his poems to Miss Fenwick, he told her that "nothing was more difficult for me in childhood than to admit the notion of death as a state applicable to my own being," and that he had written *We are Seven* to illustrate this as a common difficulty. He added :

"it was not so much from the source of animal vivacity that *my* difficulty came as from a sense of the indomitableness of the spirit within me. I used to brood over the stories of Enoch and Elijah, and almost to persuade myself that, whatever might become of others, I should be translated in something of the same way to heaven. With a feeling congenial to this, I was often unable to think of external things as having external existence, and I communed with all that I saw as something not apart from, but inherent in, my own immaterial nature."

This instinct of the child – a hardly resistible tendency rather – to pretence, to see himself and the world in the likenesses of each other and of other things,

> As if his whole vocation
> Were endless imitation,

and the subsequent profounder instinct, when bewildered and "beset with images," to resist the tendency and to see things "as they are," are the prime origins of poetry. They belong to the habit of mind which, when articulate, embodies its findings in simile and metaphor, and searches back through these towards the truth. A time was to come when Wordsworth accepted the

Bw

reality of death as the close of life ; and with it, we must suppose, he accepted the externality of the world. But he had been more closely face to face with both since the day when, " chasing the wing'd butterfly " through the green courts of Cockermouth Castle, he found himself suddenly in a dungeon whose " soul-appalling darkness " first made his " young thoughts acquainted with the grave." Wordsworth was convinced that all children are naturally poets, and that they lose the power only through the habit of the world. Hence his undying gratitude to the education which enabled him both to retain and increase his own innate glory.

Fear, next to the affection of his mother and sister, was the most important influence in the shaping of his mind, and it often shot across the " coarser pleasures " of his boyhood, and their " glad animal movements," leaving a permanent mark. The earliest of the famous " spots of time " concerned an experience of fear. When he was barely six years old his father's servant James took him out from Penrith to give him a riding lesson. They made towards the hills, but had not gone far when somehow William got separated from the man. Dismounting in his fear he led the horse across rough stony ground, when he came upon the remains of a gibbet where in former times a murderer had been hung, and the murderer's name was cut large in the grass. Turning away he went back up the common, and saw ahead of him a bleak pool between the hills, the summit crowning them, and a girl with a pitcher on her head forcing her way against the wind. " It was in truth," he said,⁻

> An ordinary sight ; but I should need
> Colours and words that are unknown to man
> To paint the visionary dreariness . . .

which lived vividly with him in his mind for ever after, leaving an extraordinary power behind it.

His first lessons were learnt partly in the Grammar School of Cockermouth ; and partly in a dame-school at Penrith when he was living there with his mother's family, the Cooksons. It was in the dame-school that he first met Mary Hutchinson, his future wife. But when Mrs. Wordsworth died, in 1778, the father, who never quite recovered from his loss, found that the management of his children as well as of his business was beyond him. Richard and William were sent away to school at Hawkshead, where the younger brothers, John and Christopher, later followed them ; and Dorothy was put into the care of her Aunt Elizabeth Threlkald at Halifax. This was the beginning of the long separation which drew from Dorothy her often repeated cry, " How we are squandered abroad ! "

For William the change was the best fortune he could have enjoyed. Every moment of his nine years at Hawkshead seemed, at least in recollection, to have contributed riches to the formation of his mind. He concurred entirely with the system which forced him

> to stand up
> Amid conflicting passions, and the shock
> Of various tempers, to endure and note
> What was not understood though known to be ;
> Among the mysteries of love and hate,
> Honour and shame, looking to right and left,

Uncheck'd by innocence too delicate
And moral-notions too intolerant,
Sympathies too contracted.

This self-dependence was confirmed when his
father died, in the winter holidays of 1783, and
he found to his surprise that though " the props
of my affection were remov'd . . . yet the building
stood, as if sustain'd by its own spirit " ; and that
the mind, his own sole and private possession,
lay open to a more intimate communion with the
visible world.

The free Grammar School at Hawkshead, near
the head of Esthwaite Water, was founded in the
sixteenth century by Archbishop Sandys of York,
and was flourishing in Wordsworth's time as one
of the best schools in the North of England. There
were several changes of master while Wordsworth
was there, but the one with whom he became a
most close friend, and who formed part of the
composite portrait " Matthew " in the poems
written many years later, was William Taylor,
who died at the age of thirty-two after serving
there for four years. The school building, which
stood just below the church, provided no accommodation for the boys who came from a distance,
and these were boarded in the village cottages.
Anne Tyson, the dame who looked after Wordsworth, and the winter nights by her fireside, are
vividly described in *The Prelude*.

School lasted for some seven or eight hours a
day (including the period for preparation), and
during them the pupils received an excellent
education. For the rest of their existence they
were completely free, without any restrictions

whatsoever. Wordsworth gave himself up entirely
to the natural amenities which surrounded him.
Skating by starlight on their lake, racing for an
island on Windermere in summer, fishing in every
pool and stream of the country, nutting in the
hazel woods, galloping over the sands of Furness,
poaching for woodcock on frosty nights, hanging
from the rocks above the raven's nest – so the
time passed in the absolute joy of Nature, who
still ministered to his gentleness with fearful shapes
and sounds, projections of his young guilt. Slowly
the glad animal days passed into ones of a deeper
ecstasy, and life was lived according to a more
regular and calculating scheme. Suddenly there
would dart across the giddiness of his pleasures
" gleams like the flashing of a shield." Soon he
learnt to hear " the ghostly language of the
ancient earth," and drank thence " the visionary
power." He went in sober search of beauty, in
solitude, or, better, in friendship. Often before
breakfast he would make the five-mile circuit of
the lake in the company of John Fleming, " then
passionately lov'd," and in the transport of beauty
and happiness lost his identity in the outer world ;
for

> such a holy calm
> Did overspread my soul, that I forgot
> That I had bodily eyes, and what I saw
> Appeared like something in myself, a dream,
> A prospect in my mind.

On those same walks at sunrise, with the same
friend, the poetry of words first entered him. As
they murmured together their " favourite verses
with one voice," he discovered the charm

Of words in tuneful order, found them sweet
For *their own sakes*, a passion and a power.

It is of singular interest that the first poems which
he wrote himself " were a task imposed by my
master " ; and when the second centenary of the
school's foundation was celebrated in 1785 he
composed, at Taylor's request, the extraordinarily
accomplished and prophetic couplets known as
the *School Exercise* ; " which put it into my head,"
he wrote, more than sixty years later, " to compose
verses from the impulse of my own mind."

In 1787 his guardians decided to send him to
Cambridge. They had great difficulty in raising
the money for him, as Lord Lonsdale, " eccentric
to the verge of madness," had seized the children's
fortune, such as it was, on the death of their
father, and justice was helpless in face of his
authority. They remained without any access to
their inheritance for nearly twenty years, until
on his father's death the son paid the debt back
with interest.

On his first arrival at Cambridge, Wordsworth's
spirit surrendered unquestioningly to the novelties
of so strange a world. He was " the dreamer," he
said, they " the dream." He provided himself
with appropriately " splendid " clothes and with
all the " other signs of manhood which supplied
the lack of beard " – thus gravely he mocked his
youthfulness in later years – and the weeks
hurried by in a round of parties. The whole
business of lectures and examinations he soon
dismissed from his mind for what it was worth,
and had only too much cause to deplore the
utter laughableness, the doting indignity of " men

unscour'd, grotesque in character," who were appointed to be his pastors and masters. What a shame in the contrast he saw, but what a lesson to be learnt from the image that flashed upon him of the true shepherds in the hills from which he had come ! Many times in his life he was to receive through such contrasts the confirmation of an original instinct. In separation from a loved object he learnt through the survival of his love the greatness of its value. If, at Cambridge, there were times when he almost risked being carried away in the common tide of life, his profound sense of values was ever at hand to restore him — either through the sense of the historic past which haunted him, and could not let him pass unmoved among the courts where Chaucer, Spenser, Milton, had once been, or through a still more deeply founded sense that he possessed a spirit which was greater than the world it was living in, a detachment from it that left a " strangeness " in his mind,

A feeling that I was not for that hour,
Nor for that place.

" The surfaces of artificial life," the exquisite sophistications of a world which he now knew for the first time, were hardly noticed by him. But, without losing for a moment his secret integrity, he could share with ease the thoughtlessness that surrounded him, and " slipp'd into the weekday works of youth," drifting aimlessly with his companions about the town, reading " lazily in lazy books," and making an extravagant riot of riding, sailing, and the rest. But when he withdrew by himself into the fields, he perceived how the vision of his childhood was expanding ; for the familiar and constant mountains being no more before his eyes, his mind, coming into contact with a new unassociated scene, turned in upon itself to examine more consciously the manner of his thoughts ; and he recognised in himself for the first time

                 visitings
Of the Upholder of the tranquil Soul,
Which underneath all passion lives secure
A steadfast life.

He perceived, too, a like moral life in every insensate detail of the surrounding world, and for the first time declared his faith in an Immanence which gave life to the whole.

When he returned to Hawkshead for his first summer vacation he consciously returned to Nature. With breathless delight he saluted all the familiar things of his loved home – the rooms, the court, the brook, the garden – and Dame Tyson took him back with a pride in him equal to his own happiness. But the change in himself left the familiar things themselves not quite the same. The greater world he had seen sent him back to the humbleness of rustic life with greater love. The woodman, the shepherd, Dame Tyson herself, drew from him a new gentleness ; and when he saw babies grown into children, and beauty fallen away from girls, and empty places where old men had basked in the sun, he seemed to have witnessed visibly the very movement of Time.

Yet he was perplexed later to balance what he had gained against what he had lost. For " a swarm of heady thoughts jostling each other "

possessed him, and the social life of " feast and
dance and public revelry " which claimed him
was too seductive a proof of his having grown up
to be resisted. It was a complete change from
his former simplicities, and he noted how

> The very garments that I wore appear'd
> To prey upon my strength, and stopp'd the course
> And quiet stream of self-forgetfulness.

In a word, he had become sophisticated. But he
needed no tragic gesture to strip the vanity away
from him, and it was again after such an occasion
that the force of contrast turned the scene to
critical advantage. He had spent the night in
a neighbouring farm at one of the wildest of those
medley dances, when love-making and midnight
madness had stretched his spirit to the utmost.
Overflowing with absurd joy, he broke away, when
cockcrow was past and the sun already up, to
walk the two miles home through the fields.

Magnificent

> The morning was, in memorable pomp,
> More glorious than I ever had beheld.
> The Sea was laughing at a distance ; all
> The solid Mountains were as bright as clouds,
> Grain-tinctured, drench'd in empyrean light ;
> And, in the meadows and the lower grounds,
> Was all the sweetness of a common dawn,
> Dews, vapours, and the melody of birds,
> And Labourers going forth into the fields.
> — Ah ! need I say, dear Friend, that to the brim
> My heart was full ; I made no vows, but vows
> Were then made for me ; bond unknown to me
> Was given, that I should be, else sinning greatly,
> A dedicated Spirit. On I walk'd
> In blessedness, which even yet remains.

CHAPTER II

1789–1795

WILLIAM was eighteen when he received this dedication. Already at an early age he seems to have detected a superior spirit within him ; from now on he set himself to use it with profit. Poetry was to be the means to this end, though he was constantly depressed by the seeming frailty of the means he had chosen. Compared with the enduring speech of earth and heaven the things which Man has wrought " for commerce of his nature with itself," however worthy of " unconquerable life," were tragically perishable.

> Tremblings of the heart
> It gives, to think that the immortal being
> No more shall need such garments ; and yet Man,
> As long as he shall be the Child of Earth,
> Might almost " weep to have " what he may lose.
> . . . Oh ! why hath not the mind
> Some element to stamp her image on
> In nature somewhat nearer to her own ?
> Why, gifted with such powers to send abroad
> Her spirit, must it lodge in shrines so frail ?

Once he had put away such wayward thoughts as these he achieved his resolution with singular ease and certainty. The difficulties were to arise when he had to choose a way of life in which poetry was possible. Even in his early days at Cambridge he had qualms that he might not be responding in the proper way to the efforts of his guardians on his behalf, and every term made his " future worldly maintenance " a more urgent question. When he returned to the university, not without regret for the autumn beauty of the mountains he was leaving and for the fun he had been having with the " frank-hearted maids of rocky Cumberland," he began his second year still without any settled plan in his work ; but, finding less amusement to be derived from " indolent and vague society," he withdrew into his own life of feeling and reflection.

It was in those days that the idea of authorship began to seem a less presumptuous one, a more real possibility ; he dared even to believe that eventually he

might leave
Some monument behind me which pure hearts
Should reverence.

At the same time he came to realise that the thinking mind was capable of complications, and the whole business of being a poet involved perplexities which it would not be easy to bear. Fortunately he soon discovered a reliable and delightful antidote in the subject of pure mathematics.

Mighty is the charm
Of those abstractions to a mind beset
With images, and haunted by itself ;
And specially delightful unto me

> Was that clear Synthesis built up aloft
> So gracefully, even then when it appear'd
> No more than as a plaything, or a toy
> Embodied to the sense, not what it is
> In verity, an independent world
> Created out of pure Intelligence.

During his second summer vacation (1789) he made various wanderings on foot. The walks in the neighbourhood of Penrith with Dorothy and Mary Hutchinson which, in *The Prelude* (Book VI), he assigns to this time, must have taken place the summer before when he was at Hawkshead, since Dorothy had removed to Forncett in Norfolk the previous December, where she remained for about four years. It is likely, however, that he did this summer rove through Dovedale and the Yorkshire Dales as he says; in which case it is possible that Mary Hutchinson, whose home was at Sockburn, near Darlington, may have accompanied him. At any rate his first interest in her must date from one of these two summers, and a gently romantic happiness coloured their times together. Of the long absence which had separated him from Dorothy he said that it made her seem " a gift then first bestowed." Then, too, the dream of a life spent together was first shared between them.

During his third summer vacation Wordsworth paid the first of many visits to the Continent. Wandering, he says (in the Fenwick note to *The Excursion*), was always his passion; and he acknowledges that in the character of the Pedlar he had represented " an idea of what I fancied my own character might have become in the circumstances." Poverty prevented him at any

time from carrying out his travels in the manner
of the "Grand Tourist" ; and no one was more
contemptuous of the conventional " search for the
picturesque." But it must not be forgotten that
in his capacity as Continental Traveller he was
sharing a fashionable inheritance and was at one
with the Spirit of the Age. It is only in this light
that a great body of his poetry can be valued.
The *Descriptive Sketches* (dating from 1790), the
Memorials of a Tour on the Continent (1820), and of a
Tour in Italy (1837), to which may be added the
Memorials of the two Scotch Tours (1803 and
1814), of the *Tour in the Summer of 1833*, the two
river-sequences of *Duddon* and *Yarrow*, together
with a mass of other topographical poetry – and a
majority of his poems have a topographical
structure – all this work belongs to a very particular genre. An exact parallel for it may be
found in contemporary painting ; in the water-
colour sketchbook records made by such men as
Turner and Cozens on their foreign travels, and
the series of descriptive views – of rivers and
properties – popular at home. Wordsworth's
travel poems abound in his usual craftsmanship,
and the pictures could have been seen by no eyes
but his own ; but for the most part their incidental
commemorative character is evident.

William's journey in the company of Robert
Jones, a fellow-collegian, amounted to a flagrant
defiance of what was expected of him. True he
had given up " all thoughts of a fellowship," but
he had not yet taken his degree. His indifference
may well have been due in part to the vagueness
of the system itself. " There will be no necessity
for me to be in Cambridge before the 10th of

November," he writes. However, he avoided
seeing his brother Richard on his way through
Town, " because he, as many of our friends at
Cambridge did, would look upon our scheme as
mad and impracticable." They landed in Calais
on July 13th, and got back there just three months
later. The interval had been spent in exhaustive
sight-seeing, almost entirely upon foot and with
barely a day's rest. Their itinerary took them
right across France to Châlons (two weeks) ;
thence by boat down the Saône to Lyons ; from
there to the Lake of Geneva, and on across the
Simplon into Italy (Como and Maggiore), followed by wanderings all round Switzerland. At
Basle, towards the end of September, they bought
a boat, and spent a week floating down the Rhine
to Cologne, and from there they returned to
Calais. The plan was thoroughly original, and
chiefly in the way it was carried out. It is possible
that they were the first undergraduates to spend
a vacation in such a manner.

" Our appearance," he writes to Dorothy, in the
charming prose of the period, " is singular ; and we
have often observed, that, in passing through a village,
we have excited a general smile. Our coats, which we
had made light on purpose for the journey, are of the
same piece ; and our manner of carrying our bundles,
which is upon our heads, with each an oak stick in
our hands, contributes not a little to that general
curiosity which we seem to excite."

He planned this journey as " a perfect enthusiast
in my admiration of Nature in all her various
forms." But it happened that, entering France
" on the very eve of that great federal day," they
found a country

> standing on the top of golden hours,
> And human nature seeming born again.

League after league, as they journeyed on high roads and in sequestered villages, they saw the nation transfigured in the radiant happiness of the Revolution. The spectacle of so intense and universal a joy broke on the Englishmen with the knowledge that there was a greater power in humanity than they had ever suspected. For another two years, however, Wordsworth's love of Nature was to prevail over human interests. He was touched by what he witnessed, " but with no intimate concern " ; and so he continued on his way to the Alps.

In many religions and philosophies of the world the ascent of a mountain – of Mt. Kailas, for example, or Mt. Sinai – has a holy significance, because the climbing of a mountain is the most apt, and, in itself, the most lovely, symbol of the achievement of a vision. Wordsworth was born almost within view of " distant Skiddaw's lofty height," his education was among mountains, and they were the natural images for his thoughts. His use of them in the account of visionary experience is the more fresh because his concern is with a reality out of which the symbol unobtrusively grows. He was the closest and most scientific observer in the comparative criticism of Nature who had lived up to that time, and his *Guide to the Lakes* is a model essay in exact appreciation of local character. He writes there, in his interesting comparison of the Alps with the mountains of Cumberland, that " the sense of sublimity depends more upon form and relation

of objects to each other than upon their actual
magnitude " ; and the objective quality which he
believed mountains possessed as a positive influence over a man's mind was the enduring
rhythm of their lines.   One of the finest passages
in *The Prelude* develops, through the power of
imagination, the description of an ascent into an
epitome of visionary striving.   They had been
ascending the Simplon Pass, steadily and serenely,
for some hours, till at last they lost the way in the
desire still to ascend, and a Peasant whom they
met had difficulty in forcing them to the knowledge that their path now led downwards.

> Loth to believe what we so grieved to hear,
> For still we had hopes that pointed to the clouds,[1]
> We questioned him again, and yet again ;
> But every word that from the peasant's lips
> Came in reply, translated by our feelings,
> Ended in this, – *that we had crossed the Alps*.

It was one of the " spots of time " which opened
to him the gates of infinity, as surely as the pilgrim
of Kailas found himself in the presence of his God ;
and it summoned from him a great cry of exalta-
tion.

> Imagination ! lifting up itself
> Before the eye and progress of my Song
> Like an unfather'd vapour ; here that Power,
> In all the might of its endowments, came
> Athwart me ; I was lost as in a cloud,
> Halted, without a struggle to break through.
> And now recovering, to my Soul I say

---

[1] This line, which sums up the point of the story, occurs only
in the 1850 text, and is a good example of the greater precision
and clarity sometimes found in the later version.   (Except when
otherwise stated, quotations from *The Prelude* will be made
from the 1805 text.)

I recognise thy glory; in such strength
Of usurpation, in such visitings
Of awful promise, when the light of sense
Goes out in flashes that have shewn to us
The invisible world, doth Greatness make abode,
There harbours whether we be young or old.
Our destiny, our nature, and our home
Is with infinitude, and only there ;
With hope it is, hope that can never die,
Effort, and expectation, and desire,
And something evermore about to be.

When they had brought themselves to descend
from that eminence they travelled down the Pass
in the serene and serious wisdom which succeeds
such a transport, knowing that

       The immeasurable height
Of woods decaying, never to be decay'd,
The stationary blasts of water-falls,
And every where along the hollow rent
Winds thwarting winds, bewilder'd and forlorn,
The torrents shooting from the clear blue sky,
The rocks that muttered close upon our ears,
Black drizzling crags that spake by the way-side
As if a voice were in them, the sick sight
And giddy prospect of the raving stream,
The unfetter'd clouds, and region of the Heavens,
Tumult and peace, the darkness and the light
Were all like workings of one mind, the features
Of the same face, blossoms upon one tree,
Characters of the great Apocalypse,
The types and symbols of Eternity,
Of first and last, and midst, and without end.

Such a store of riches did his mind take up in
every place. The " impassion'd sight of colours
and of forms " left their beauty with him, and
the transports he suffered left him " not rich one

Cw

moment to be poor for ever," but with an emotion to be recollected at any fitting time that would give back not to himself only, but to all men for ever, the riches again with increase.

He visited Dorothy that Christmas at Forncett ; it was the last occasion they were to see each other for three years. He took his degree in January, but, being still quite irresolute in the matter of a profession, he chose to spend some time in London. There he finally proved for himself, through the austere power of memory, the value of the standards with which Nature had provided him. It was the recollection of the steadfast order of the mountains that preserved him from the futility which overwhelms those who live

> amid the same perpetual flow
> Of trivial objects, melted and reduced
> To one identity, by differences
> That have no law, no meaning, and no end.

For he, in contrast, could keep his mind strong with the support of fixed unchanging images

> By influence habitual to the mind
> The mountain's outline and its steady form
> Gives a pure grandeur, and its presence shapes
> The measure and the prospect of the soul
> To majesty.

And so this talisman of memory allowed him to revel to his heart's content in all that the City provided, without his needing the blind anger of satire to save himself from its corruption. A far surer detachment was lodged within him ; and thus it came about that the great poet of Nature was in that very capacity the one best fitted to give a truly poetic account of the City. Hardly even the novelists have described with so much meaning in their zest such a London as Wordsworth gives in the seventh book of *The Prelude*. Rejoicing in detail for its own sake – and there, again, having the advantage of a stranger that everything was fresh to him – he crowds into his lines the whole " motley imagery " of that rushing world from the daily street scene to the fantasy of Bartholomew Fair ; from the life of the River, Westminster, St. Paul's, Parliament, and the Pulpit, the Courts, to all its most curious entertainments – Theatres, Circuses, Panoramas, and Pantomime ; and all these things combined at once in the place he loved and frequented most – " Half-rural Sadler's Wells," which later became again curiously linked to him and his country when they produced there a melodrama, *Mary of Buttermere*, the sad story of the daughter of a publican in a neighbouring vale who was well known to him and Coleridge and De Quincey. She was wooed and married by one who soon turned out to be an adventuring bigamist and forger, circumstances which secured for her the lively interest of the entire nation.[1]

Even that restless triviality which he notes so carefully served to deepen his thought ; for he felt that it was

[1] The narration, which takes up some space in the book, and leads him on to other associated things, is far from being, as is sometimes said, an irrelevant discursion, but is rather a skilfully devised and well-timed reminder *via* the medium of Sadler's Wells of another different world. *Mary of Buttermere*, by T. Dibdin, belongs to the genre of "The Natural Child," which was the most curiously recurrent theme in the drama of the day. Wordsworth, who had a personal interest in the matter, often refers to this urgent and fashionable problem.

> not to be despis'd
> By those who have observ'd the curious props
> By which the perishable hours of life
> Rest on each other, and the world of thought
> Exists and is sustain'd,

an early instance of the genius for realism which increased in him with years. The men are few who, being wise enough to detect

> all the strife of singularity,
> Lies to the ear, and lies to every sense,

can go a step further and accept them as

> a common produce, things that are
> To-day, to-morrow will be, [take] of them
> Such willing note as, on some errand bound
> Of pleasure or of Love some Traveller might,
> Among a thousand other images,
> Of sea-shells that bestud the sandy beach,
> Or daisies swarming through the fields in June.

But what most disturbed him in those days was indeed the greatest mystery he ever faced, the modern mystery which the novelists of our own times have pursued with special interest – the attempt which each man must make to believe in the identity of other men independent of himself. " How often," wrote Wordsworth, addressing himself specially to Coleridge –

> How often in the overflowing Streets,
> Have I gone forward with the Crowd, and said
> Unto myself, the face of every one
> That passes by me is a mystery,

and when he saw a blind beggar wearing a written paper to explain his story, he related how

My mind did at this spectacle turn round
As with the might of waters, and it seem'd
To me that in this Label was a type,
Or emblem, of the utmost that we know,
Both of ourselves and of the universe.

And so, as the strange mysterious stream of name-less people passed him in the streets, the new great love of humanity began to grow in his mind.

In April he became twenty-one. He spent most of the summer in Wales with Robert Jones, happy, but still oppressed with the sense of indolence ; and the craving to wander, from which all his life he was never free, almost obsessed him now. But his frank distaste for the dependence on others which that would certainly involve restrained him, and, writing to his friend Mathews, who shared the longing, he said :

Were we in possession of perhaps even less than a hundred a year apiece, which would amply obviate the objection I have just made, and without any relations to whom we were accountable, I would set out with you this moment with all my heart.

Long afterwards he realised gratefully that if it had been possible for him to become a wanderer he would never have become a poet.

An uncle seems then to have urged him to take Holy Orders, and his cousin Jack Robinson offered him a curacy, which he was fortunately able to refuse with the excuse of being two years too young for admission to Orders. It was not always so easy for his mind to provide reasons for deferring decision. He spent the autumn at Cambridge in response to his uncle's new proposal that he should begin the study of Oriental Languages – an

" immense wilderness " from which he provided his own escape by arranging his departure to France, his professed intention being to perfect his French as qualification for a tutorship.

He crossed from Brighton to Dieppe at the end of November, and after halting for a few days in Paris, where the scenes of new history and the dust of the Bastille first attracted his slowly-waking interest to the Revolution, he travelled on to his destination at Orléans, chosen perhaps for no more definite reason than the beauty of the country and the purity of its speech.

He was slow to feel the excitement of the new France, because, as he explains, there was little in it new to him. He had read Rousseau, but without surprise. For by the supreme favour of his birth – and his constant gratitude for it impresses us as proof of sincerity – he had grown up in a world where the conditions and policies of republican thought were the order of the day. Cambridge continued those conditions for him ; and he had to learn what other thought in other worlds might be before he could know that his was a state worth fighting for.

By a noteworthy chance his first associates at Orléans were Royalists – a band of military officers, desperate in their devotion to the lost cause – and a girl with whom he fell in love. Thus it was once more through a contrast that he learnt the value of his beliefs ; and when, with sudden passionate pride, he adopted the name of patriot and gave his heart to the people, he suffered no change in himself, but had found simply that the cast of his mind could find its reflection in another mirror than the still lakes

of his home ; the same image was thrown back by
the great seas of revolution.

In fact he witnessed his original and natural
ideas proved in the necessity of action ; and it was
by friendship with

> one whom circumstance
> Hath call'd upon to embody his deep sense
> In action, give it outwardly a shape —

the noble and ever-remembered Captain Michel
Beaupuy, that Wordsworth entered elate into the
spirit of the movement itself. With him his
political judgments were more sound, because
more practical " than afterwards " — he confesses
so himself — when, removed from contact with
the events themselves, he was led into the excesses
of Godwinism ; while now, with Beaupuy at his
side, he carried with him

> With less alloy to its integrity
> The experience of past ages.

For Wordsworth he was a hero, the first of the
" Happy Warriors " in the admiration of whom
much in his own character was formed.

> Injuries
> Made him more gracious, and his nature then
> Did breathe its sweetness out most sensibly
> As aromatic flowers on alpine turf
> When foot hath crush'd them. He thro' the events
> Of that great change wander'd in perfect faith,
> As through a Book, an old Romance or Tale
> Of Fairy, or some dream of actions wrought
> Behind the summer clouds. By birth he rank'd
> With the most noble, but unto the poor
> Among mankind he was in service bound
> As by some tie invisible, oaths profess'd
> To a religious Order.

Together they wandered in the country of the Loire, their argument passing from the abstract themes of God and Man to the immediate problems of the rights of man in their present world ; finding everywhere in the scenes of the place matter for the expression of their thoughts ; whether in the heart-rending spectacle of the "hunger-bitten" girl dragging a heifer, or in the violated châteaux testifying to the overthrow of that "absolute rule where will of One is law for all."

But even with the man of action at his side he found himself tempted back into his world of reverie – just as his poetic seclusion was so often to be agitated by his longing to be an actor in the outer world. So that the very ruins which symbolised the victory of revolution were themselves the best pictures of the romance which enthralled him; for the violent excitements of the times, and the deep love into which he had fallen, coincided with his first serious devotion to poetry. He was at work upon the *Descriptive Sketches*, recounting in heroic couplets his Alpine Tour of two years earlier with Jones, in which the most remarkable feature biographically is the way his earlier mood is coloured over with his present melancholy. The diction is made out of the dignified artifices which he was shortly to reject as vicious, but the observation of Nature was so new, and its expression sometimes so striking, that Coleridge, who read the poem when it was published the following year, declared that "seldom, if ever, was the emergence of an original poetic genius above the literary horizon more evidently announced."

Meanwhile he was in love. Annette Vallon

whom he met in the house of acquaintances at
Orléans, where she was staying, was the daughter
of a surgeon at Blois, and four years older than
William. Some members of her family seem at
least to have accepted the Revolution, but, after
her brother Paul had run into great danger early
the following year, she proclaimed herself a
violent Royalist, and ran into equal dangers
herself for that cause. It may be noted at once
that love, the only effective changer of opinions,
did not change theirs – William remained Republican, Annette increased in Royalism. But in
the beginning opinions could stand aside (though
when he told the story, in *Vaudracour and Julia*,
he introduced an opposition of parents separating
the lovers which was perhaps intended to repre-
sent an equivalent external circumstance). The
world was well lost in the beginning of their
passion, and but for Beaupuy it might have been
lost altogether. The lines in which he com-
memorated his happiness are among the most
radiant passages of love-poetry.

> Earth liv'd in one great presence of the spring,
> Life turn'd the meanest of her implements
> Before his eyes to price above all gold,
> The house she dwelt in was a sainted shrine,
> Her chamber-window did surpass in glory
> The portals of the East, all paradise
> Could by the simple opening of a door
> Let itself in upon him, pathways, walks,
> Swarm'd with enchantment till his spirit sank
> Beneath the burden, overbless'd for life.

She conceived a child ; and it is sufficient to
imagine what prolonged wretchedness the event
must have brought with it. Tempting as it is to

reconstruct a psychological development in the poet from the event, the evidence is altogether too inadequate, and such as exists is open to interpretations too various, to warrant such a proceeding. But it is legitimate to note the absolute consistency of the episode with the rest of his behaviour. Wordsworth was born a child of violent natural passions. De Quincey wrote of him : " Wordsworth's intellectual passions were fervent and strong : but they rested upon a basis of preternatural animal sensibility diffused through *all* the animal passions (or appetites) " ; and he notes that this is in more or less degree true of all poets who were " great by original force and power." A conflict between sensualism and asceticism is the prevailing condition in English poetry. Of Wordsworth it is abundantly proved both by what he writes about himself in his poetry and by the nature of the poetry itself. His passion was so exceptional that it threatened even in his childhood to overwhelm him. The great fact of his genius was that he realised at once the necessity of controlling himself with an equal power. In no other way would the continuance of life have been possible for him. His success was heroic. It was also exhausting ; and if in a period of his later – though not latest – life we observe a certain intolerance in his thought and ways, we have only to remember that it was his final measure against the world of Nature which continued to assail him.

His love of Annette was the only passion which failed to be met with an equal disciplinary power ; and his nephew and first biographer was perhaps after all near the truth in assigning the cause to the condition of the time. "The most licentious theories were propounded; all restraints were broken; libertinism was law." He recovered very soon, and so, perhaps, when her genuine pain had given place to a fashionable sensibility, did she. The course of his life progressed from now slowly on to his rest in "the depth and not the tumult of the soul"; and after ten years his wife brought to him that utter stillness in himself which was his great strength both as poet and man.

He had passed the spring and summer between Blois and Orléans, and was in the latter town when on September 21st the Convention was opened. His money was running very low, and on this account he made for Paris in October, where he (presumably) delayed in the hope of obtaining help from home; and finally was "compelled by nothing less than absolute want of funds" to return to England before the end of the year, although on December 15th Annette had given birth to his daughter. Again in this he was able, later, to see the hand of Providence. For the Terror was just breaking over France, and it seems certain that Wordsworth's activities had been sufficiently compromising to have involved him in a profitless and silly death. On January 21st the King was executed, and on February 1st France declared war on England. William and Annette were enemies, and there was no knowing how long the separation might be.

When he came to refer to the story of his love, in the poem of the Growth of his Mind, he did so in the form of a nearly, but not quite, parallel narrative of another pair of unhappy lovers, Vaudracour and Julia, which had been told him by Beaupuy. A number of perhaps not too fanciful things are suggested by this, among them that Beaupuy had been made his confessor and had used as one means of consolation the fact that William was not the only person to whom such things had occurred (and he certainly was not ; the drama of the day seems to have no other subject for discussion). Beaupuy in the end would have been a more lasting influence than Annette herself. And after ten years, perhaps, the whole episode came to seem so much a dream, a story which belonged so little to his present self, that it was truer to relate it in the terms of fiction. In some parts of the story, especially the insanity of the hero which concludes it, and which departs apparently from the story of the original Vaud-racour, one cannot but feel that Wordsworth is giving expression to a morbid anxiety-fantasy about himself, indulging some of the " fond and wayward thoughts " to which he was so prone. We know from other contexts of his pleasure in inventing characters to describe himself as he might have been.

Both the outer circumstances of the next three years (1793–95) and the movements of his mind remain obscure, but they seem rather to have been a break in the continuity of his growth than a vital part of it. His flight into heresies was temporary, and when at its conclusion his sister Dorothy led him gently back to the world where he belonged, he re-entered the security of his true beliefs with quieter and more serious passion ; for his suffering had been extreme. He confided in her now, and she accepted Annette, but the only result of her brave attempt to plead for

William with her uncle was the order that they should not meet.

He finally dropped the plan of obtaining a curacy, which, less for itself than as a means of marrying Annette, he had continued to entertain. Dorothy at once began to correspond with Annette, and continued to do so as regularly as William, or more so, but the confiscation of letters made the attempt almost useless. Such of Annette's as reached them were so piteous that William – it is now generally believed – made a desperate attempt to reach her, and actually got through to Paris in October, but was unable to proceed further. During the summer he had spent a month of calm and glassy days in the Isle of Wight, waiting for his opportunity which never came then; but he watched in despair the naval preparations for war. The Revolution itself had been to him " nothing out of Nature's second course "; now his first great crisis was come.

> No shock
> Given to my moral nature had I known
> Down to that very moment; neither lapse
> Nor turn of sentiment that might be nam'd
> A revolution, save at this one time,
> All else was progress on the self-same path
> On which with a diversity of pace
> I had been travelling; this a stride at once
> Into another region.

The two fundamental parts of Wordsworth's mind were his belief in Nature and his faith in the people (who, as far as he knew them, enjoyed a privileged relationship towards Nature). Both of these expressed themselves powerfully in his patriotic love of England; his mind's inheritance was her very soil, its companions were her labourers. But this patriotism, particularly on its human side, had become extended to France; and personal love had sealed the bond. The oneness of England and France was the very integrity of his mind. And suddenly a senseless, irresponsible war had destroyed it; he

felt

> The ravage of this most unnatural strife
> In my own heart.

He did not break down at once, but for several months more struggled to preserve the separate parts of his belief intact. He defended the Revolution in a reply to a sermon by a recanting bishop – Watson of Llandaff – one who had formerly seemed to bless the event. Wordsworth's logic is as forceful as his contempt, and his work remains a useful contribution to Socialism. The extreme, and perhaps justified, caution of brother Richard may have been the reason for the work's remaining in manuscript,[1] and its chief purpose was accomplished in the writing of it.

Nature, he found, still possessed him with delight when he journeyed from the Island across England. On Salisbury Plain the vestiges of antiquity drew him into a strange visionary

[1] First published 1876. On the subject of the bishop's apparently double-minded attitude to Reform, Wordsworth writes: "In some parts of England it is quaintly said, when a drunken man is seen reeling towards his home, that he has business on both sides of the road. Observing your lordship's tortuous path, the spectators will be far from insinuating that you have partaken of Mr. Burke's intoxicating bowl; they will content themselves, shaking their heads as you stagger along, with remarking that you have business on both sides of the road." The passage is a pleasant example of the aptitude of his imagery, in whatever medium he was writing; and also of the humour in which he is popularly supposed to have been deficient.

reverie in which he realised with an astonishing force his historical inheritance, and " that Poets, even as Prophets, each with each " are " connected in a mighty scheme of truth." Their torch had been placed in his hands, the dedication of that morning five years ago was confirmed in this moment, and he humbly accepted that the work which it lay in him to produce " might become a power like one of Nature's." He travelled on alone towards Wales, and came to the valley of the Wye. He saw Tintern Abbey for the first time ; and its beauty possessed him so entirely that its name must be linked for ever with the deepest experiences of mankind. On that day

> when like a roe
> I bounded o'er the mountains, by the sides
> Of the deep rivers, and the lonely streams,
> Wherever nature led,

the whole force of his unthinking joy in the scene was gathered up into his memory entire, so that when after five years the scene itself came once more before his eyes, he built upon it the poem in which every part of his feeling and thought is concentrated. From Tintern he travelled on to his friend Robert Jones in North Wales, and with him made the ascent of Snowdon which is so magnificently described in *The Prelude*, Book XIII (XIV) with one of his most eloquent pictures of the imaginative mind.[1]

That these three scenes occurred that summer shows that his flight from reality was neither suddenly nor lightly made. One last glory in the

[1] The picture is still more wonderfully developed in the 1850 version. Legouis assigned this excursion to the visit of 1791, but the poem itself makes the chronology quite clear.

Revolution was left to him. He had spent all the first part of the next year (1794) in the North, paying visits with Dorothy, who had escaped from Forncett ; and in August he was staying near Peele Castle – another scene that was to become the subject of one of his most imaginative recollections. As he walked one day at low tide across Ulverston Sands, with the happiest memories of childhood possessing him, the news fell on his ears that *Robespierre was dead.* It was a manifest proof of the power of republicanism to cast forth tyranny from its midst ; and he breathed forth his most thrilling Hymn of Triumph. The meaning of the words is eternal, but the occasion was a delusion. During the next months their ruthless invasions of other lands showed that the French " had become oppressors in their turn." Ironically enough their action was a fair example of Godwinian Necessity,[1] but only events abroad were visible to Wordsworth, not the domestic necessity which had dictated them ; and with every vehicle for his ideals in the form of governments collapsing behind him, he fled to the only support he could find to save himself from collapsing with them. He fell into the blessed illusion of Reason. Godwin's *Political Justice,* which appeared shortly after Wordsworth's return from France, attracted his attention then, but only in so far as it supplied confirmation for his hatred of certain social evils (especially those resulting from the war), the corollaries of his Necessitarianism. Under the influence of this part of it he composed his first considerable poem –

[1] I follow the chronological account worked out by Professor de Selincourt in his edition of *The Prelude*, p. 584.

Guilt and Sorrow. Now, a year later, the more abstract parts of the theory provided him with a timely escape from the incomprehensible history of facts. To bear the pain of his broken past, he made an almost complete reversal of the beliefs which had nourished it. Instead of observing the behaviour of man and the nature of his world, and realistically deducing laws from them, he proposed an ideal man, in an ideal world of pure reason, the very virtues of which would have the power to make themselves real. It is easy to see that so barren a philosophy, and one so discordant with his education and (*pace* Godwin) with his " innate ideas," could not hold him fast or long. Mark Rutherford shrewdly discerned in the event no intellectual conviction, but a symptom of psychological ill health. The sickness progressed away from Godwinism in a nervous scepticism which demanded *proof* of every mental judgment, till

> I lost
> All feeling of conviction, and, in fine,
> Sick, wearied out with contrarieties,
> Yielded up moral questions in despair,

and he turned once more towards the only activity whose proofs were absolute – " towards mathematics, and their clear and solid evidence."

Part of the sickness was his wretched uncertainty in the matter of a career. The need of means was desperate – but " all professions," he remarked, giving utterance to one of his most enduring, if minor, truths, " all professions are attended with great inconveniences." His friend Matthews proposed the starting of a periodical miscellany, and Wordsworth's planning of the paper is

Dw

interesting as an illustration of " that totality of
unified interests " of which, as Mr. Eliot observes,
his poetry was the expression. He never doubted
now but that he was a poet, but his paper was to
be first and foremost political ; the undertaking
would be worthless unless they were " to inculcate
principles of government and forms of social
order." A secondary item would be "critical
remarks on Poetry, etc., etc., upon the arts of
Painting, Gardening, and other subjects of amusement " upon which he also felt himself qualified to
write. The work never materialised, on account
of Wordsworth's unwilling, but inevitable, absence
from town. The surprising remark in a letter,
" Cataracts and mountains are good occasional
society, but they will not do for constant companions," suggests how the temporary sophistica-
tion of his mind was feeling the need of a town as
its proper sphere. He was too poor to run the
risk of finding himself in London unemployed ;
and he was also detained at the bedside of a sick
friend. Raisley Calvert, who lay dying at Penrith,
left one of the greatest benefactions to English
poetry. He had already with generous insight
offered Wordsworth a share in his income, and,
when he knew that death by consumption was
coming to him young, he wrote out a legacy of
£900. Wordsworth nursed him till his death in
January 1795 ; and duly recorded in *The Prelude*
how the man whose name " shall live, if words of
mine can give it life," had done this thing which

> clear'd a passage for me, and the stream
> Flowed in the bent of Nature.

CHAPTER III

1795 – 1798

Racedown – Dorothy – *The Borderers* – Coleridge – *The Ruined Cottage* – they move to Nether Stowey – Alfoxden – Thomas Poole – the walk to Lynton – plan of the *Lyrical Ballads* – differences between Wordsworth and Coleridge – *Peter Bell* – the Lyrics of Nature – Ruth – idiots and children – visits of Hazlitt and Thelwall – the spy – they leave Alfoxden – *Tintern Abbey*.

Now at long last was made real for them that dream which Dorothy had so often and so tenderly dreamed – of the secluded country cottage where their whole lives could be shared together. A few months of hesitation followed Raisley's death, during which the plan was mooted of their living in London as journalists ; but William found that the restlessness of that life was wholly uncongenial to more serious composition, and the proposal of a friend finally and fortunately closed London to him as a sphere of activity. Basil Montagu, a natural son of the Earl of Sandwich, had lost his wife, and asked William and Dorothy to undertake the charge of his small son Basil. (The natural daughter of a cousin was also to join them, but the plan fell through.) And a young Mr. Pinney of Bristol offered them a house – Racedown – near the Dorset coast.

Wordsworth set out on foot from Bristol one September afternoon, and as he made across the country towards his new home he poured forth that cry of deliverance which opens *The Prelude* – his thanksgiving at freedom achieved from all cities. " The earth is all before me," he cried, beginning

51

with Milton's ending. A gentle autumn wind fanned him, and he " felt within a corresponding mild creative breeze " which grew to a tempest. Such was its power that, though

> not used to make
> A present joy the matter of my Song,

he recorded the moment in the moment itself, without waiting for a later tranquillity. And walking on in the evening he chose that present tranquillity to summon up recollections from his past ; but the attempt to make poetry ended in silence, and

> " Be it so,
> It is an injury," said I, " to this day
> To think of anything but present joy."

Everything at Racedown shared in the work of restoration – Nature, the peasantry, and Dorothy who had never forsaken them. The passion which bound this passionate brother and sister is unknown in any other story. They had been separated for sixteen years, and now they spoke the language of lovers. In the exquisite poem of the Glow-worm, " Among all lovely things my love hath been," in which eight years later he recalled an episode from the early Race-down days, he gives her the name of Lucy[1] and talks of her as his love. And love reaches one of its furthest utterances when he speaks of her

> whom I have loved
> With such communion, that no place on earth
> Can ever be a solitude to me.

[1] He is riding a horse by night near the " Dwelling of my love." Cf. " Strange fits of passion."

And with just such a love she speaks of him in her
letters and journals. We can only see the fruit
which it bore. Its working is beyond our understanding, though we catch glimpses of its sorrows
and joys. It is certain that the idea of William's
marriage would hardly have been endurable to
her but for the fact that his chosen wife was her
own dearest friend; and it is doubtful if William
would have married under circumstances that
prevented Dorothy from being one of the household. They all lived together for nearly fifty
years without a moment of difference between
them. But no human frame, not even Dorothy's,
with its rare athletic strength, could support un-
injured the long strain of unexpressed emotion –
if, as seems likely, she loved Coleridge, her torment is doubled – and it is little wonder that her
mind at last broke beneath it. She had saved
William from the very destruction which fell
upon herself; and he knew what he owed to
those first days in which they lived together.

> Then it was
> That the belovèd Woman in whose sight
> Those days were pass'd, now speaking in a voice
> Of sudden admonition, like a brook
> That did but cross a lonely road, and now
> Seen, heard and felt, and caught at every turn,
> Companion never lost through many a league,
> Maintained for me a saving intercourse
> With my true self; for, though impair'd and chang'd
> Much, as it seemed, I was no further chang'd
> Than as a clouded, not a waning moon :
> She, in the midst of all, preserv'd me still
> A Poet, made me seek beneath that name
> My office upon earth, and nowhere else.

Even the small boy Basil contributed as much as he received ; for " he lies like a little devil," wrote William, and that and other items of natural conduct suggested the unlikelihood of man's deficiency in " innate ideas." Moreover the admirably enlightened education of him which they undertook together stimulated that interest in child-psychology which plays so important a part in William's writings. The pieces on which he was engaged may also be considered as cathartic – some not very serious satires based on Juvenal and mainly directed against kingship, and a far more significant work, his tragedy, *The Borderers*. The preface which accompanies the play is in a sense more important than the play itself, for until this was discovered[1] the intention of its complicated plot remained obscure. As Professor de Selincourt writes : " The prime weakness of *The Borderers* as a drama lies, not in the plot viewed in itself, but rather in that plot's unsuitability for making clear the central idea on which the plot is working." A performance of it might possibly suggest more clarity in the dramatic ideas than emerges from a reading. It is at any rate now established that its purpose is mainly to exhibit the dangers of trusting to reason, i.e., to expose Godwinism, though in the process of doing so, both in the preface and the play, a whole psychology of the greatest intricacy is presented, to illustrate " that constitution and those tendencies of human nature which make the apparently *motiveless* actions of bad men intelligible

[1] First printed in *The Nineteenth Century* of November 1926, with an acute commentary by Professor de Selincourt. Reprinted in his *Oxford Lectures on Poetry*, O.U.P., 1934.

to careful observers." In more than one passage he speaks the very language of modern theory; and he throws out an incidental observation which is at least as satisfactory an account of the drama as any other.

As literature, the play is interesting on various grounds. It was his first developed attempt at blank verse, and it contains some extraordinarily successful and striking passages. The influence of Shakespeare is scarcely disguised. Professor de Selincourt notes the close parallel with *Othello*; and parallels may also be noted with *Lear* – the entire setting of the climax of the play – various parts of a desolate moor, a storm, the inside of a poor cottage; with Herbert, the old father, deriving from both Gloucester and Lear; while a great number of verbal reminiscences,[1] especially from *Lear* and *Hamlet*, indicates a remarkable absorption of his models.

Of more significance is the relation of the play to contemporary literature, for it provided the first distinct signs of Wordsworth's willingness to adopt, and employ for his own purposes, the lively idiom of the day. He may claim to be the most purely original genius in our literature; but at the same time he takes his place in a well-knit development of tradition, and he had to make a rapid and useful progression from the past through the present before he could stand up as the prophet of a new movement. The manner of his early work is almost entirely retrospective. In *Guilt and Sorrow* he used the Spenserian stanza which Thomson, in 1748, had revived to a new

---

[1] The pursuit of them in detail might prove a rewarding labour.

and exciting life. Now, in *The Borderers*, he takes over the entire machinery of the Gothic Revival. Gothic literature is made up of two invariable factors – the sentimental doctrine " that truth and virtue shall succeed at last," and the setting of artificial romance and terror in which it is presented. This setting generally provides an horrific mystery often contrived with great ingenuity, which has all the appearance of a supernatural phenomenon but for which in the end a natural explanation is discovered. A much smaller class, including the *Castle of Otranto*, which may be conveniently accepted as the origin of the movement (1765), presents the supernatural as having an actual existence. (It was on a point arising out of this that Coleridge and Wordsworth had their famous disagreement.) Wordsworth, according the treatment of all ages to their immediate predecessors, believed himself to be in violent reaction against the Gothic. We see him now developing logically out of it. What he rejected in it was the distressing triviality of the greater part of the work which it produced. The idiom itself he found useful enough, but he gave it a significance which had occurred to none of its inventors. What was artificial in their romance he made real[1]; what was false in their mystery he made profound. And the sham darkness which

---

[1] One must at the same time remember how far towards meeting him some of the Gothic writers had gone. Mrs. Radcliffe produces the following remark in *The Mysteries of Udolpho* (1794), Ch. V : " St. Aubert smiled, and sighed at the romantic picture of felicity his fancy drew, and sighed again to think that Nature and simplicity were so little known to the world *as that their pleasures were romantic.*" One could hardly find a neater expression of the Wordsworthian, as opposed to the Coleridgean, attitude.

they had invented out of boredom with the light of reason became a real symbol of what is hidden from men's eyes. (An interesting example of his use of a symbol is found in the poem which is generally known by the abbreviated title *Tintern Abbey*. The Abbey itself is not mentioned once in the poem ; but by virtue of the title the picture of an ivy-clad ruin, the regular Gothic symbol for the triumph of Nature over the works of man, fittingly remains in the mind all the time.)

The same was the case with regard to the new fashion in ballads, which he turned to original use. To Johnson's attempt to refute their validity as poetry by an idiotic parody, Wordsworth's easy reply was that " the *matter* expressed in Dr. Johnson's stanza is contemptible." But that did not invalidate the method in his own practice of it. He deliberately chose the barest means, that the matter which he had to express might be free from the danger of confusion with ornament.

In *The Borderers* Wordsworth borrowed the Gothic atmosphere and scene, and even some of the sentiment, though naturally only as an ornament of the dramatic structure, not as the structure itself. But whatever stuff it be made of, Coleridge hailed it. " His drama is absolutely wonderful," he wrote. " There are in the piece those profound touches of the human heart which I find three or four times in the *Robbers* of Schiller, and often in Shakespeare ; but in Wordsworth there are no inequalities."

Thus magnificently comes Coleridge upon the scene. It is strange that the beginning of so great a friendship is not exactly known. Probably they

met through Cottle, his publisher, during Wordsworth's short visit to Bristol which immediately
precedes the opening of *The Prelude*. The excitement of that outburst may in that case owe something to the electrifying effect which Coleridge
had upon all who met him ; and, as the poem
was written specially for him, the choice of that
moment from which to start would have had a
special significance. But at any rate it was not
till eighteen months later that the event began to
develop consequences. During the early spring
of 1797 Mary Hutchinson, whose younger sister
Margaret had died of consumption, came to stay
at Racedown. Dorothy was always her greatest
friend, and there is much likelihood for supposing
that William had loved her before ever he met
Annette. In March, Montagu joined them, and
persuaded William to pay with him a two weeks'
visit to Bristol – presumably to discuss the possible
publication of *Guilt and Sorrow* with Cottle – which
William, since he could leave Dorothy and Mary
in each other's company, was willing to do.
There, doubtless, the poets met again, and it is
possible that Coleridge carried Wordsworth off
with him to his home at Nether Stowey for a few
days. In June the visit was repaid ; and to the
end of their lives they could recall the manner
of his arrival, when " he did not keep to the
high road, but leapt over a gate and bounded
down the pathless field by which he cut off an
angle."

Each of them found in the other the fulfilment
of an immediate need. Coleridge was the type of
character which finds its most fruitful expression
in the conscious submission of itself to a greater

power. Hence the distinctively religious turn of his mind; hence also his unsatisfactory relations with women, and his tremendous joy at finding in Wordsworth a human being whom he knew to be greater than himself. " Wordsworth," he wrote to Southey, " is a very great man, the only man to whom *at all times* and *in all modes of excellence* I feel myself inferior." Coleridge's life was rendered extraordinarily difficult for him by this unusual combination of the consciousness of his worth with the negative instinct to surrender himself to something greater. He had to find a friend who would recognise his greatness and at the same time direct it. By singular fortune he had met the only man in the world capable of undertaking the responsibility. Wordsworth sensed at once what was required of him. " Nothing is more curious," writes M. Legouis, " than the simplicity with which Wordsworth accepted the recognition of his superior genius, nor more admirable than the self-denying anxiety of Coleridge to undeceive his own admirers, and to make them bow down like himself before the great man he had discovered." In later years Wordsworth laboured devotedly to support his friend ; but when Coleridge removed himself from his influence, and found no one else in the world big enough to accept his surrender, the negative instinct was forced to express itself in the only other available way, self-pity.

Wordsworth addressed Coleridge as the " most loving[1] soul ! Placed on this earth to love and understand " ; and love and understanding were what he was most needing to piece together the

---

[1] " Capacious " in the 1850 version.

broken fragments of his mind. Dorothy's labour
was to bring back his mind to the objective world
– the world of ear and eye. (That was also her
part of the contribution to Coleridge, to whom the
observation of objects and the interest in trivi-
alities were not a natural gift.) The vast resources
of his intellectual genius were what he gave in
return, completing for William the work begun by
Dorothy in setting her world in new and ever-
changing lights. "He was most wonderful,"
wrote Wordsworth, long afterwards, "in the
power he possessed of throwing out in profusion
grand central truths from which might be evolved
the most comprehensive systems." The first
system which he brought with him was the
sensationalist philosophy of Hartley, to which he
then subscribed so wholly that he fastened the
name upon his new-born son, to be a constant
memorial. Hartley's system delighted Wordsworth with the confirmation it gave him of his own
instinct that the senses are our prime source of
knowledge, and it helped him to formulate the
psychology which linked the man with the child.
But he was far too much a poet to risk binding
himself to any belief that might run counter to the
sudden-darting emotion of a moment. Poetry is
never the slave of philosophy, and the attempt to
reconcile all that a poet says with any but a most
general creed is profitless. Wordsworth was himself constrained as an old man to make an explanation of the sentiments in the *Immortality* Ode which
had given pain to "some good and pious persons"; and he satisfied them by saying : "I took
hold of the notion of pre-existence as having
sufficient foundation in humanity for authorising

me to make for my purpose the best use of it I could as a Poet."

" The first thing that was read," wrote Dorothy to Mary, who had left a day or two before Coleridge leapt in upon them, " was William's new poem *The Ruined Cottage* with which he was much delighted ; and after tea he repeated to us two acts and a half of his tragedy *Osorio*. The next morning William read his tragedy *The Borderers*." Coleridge expressed himself as definitely over the new poem as he did over the play. He declared simply that it was " superior, I hesitate not to aver, to anything in our language which in any way resembles it." It became the opening of *The Excursion* for which it was perhaps already planned, but in the interval underwent some changes. It was followed by *The Old Cumberland Beggar*. One cannot fail to be struck by the enormous advance made in these two poems over *The Borderers*, especially in the sudden total disappearance of obvious literary influences, together with a simplification of language and narrative. The finished Wordsworth stands revealed. He had discovered both the choice of subject and the manner of presenting it, in which most properly to exhibit the passions of his heart ; themselves having been sorted into a clearer formulation by his observation of life at its barest among the lowliest of mankind.

What each of the friends may have owed to the other, and how far Coleridge and Dorothy fell in love with one another, are beyond our determination now. To themselves already their lives seemed so indivisible that Coleridge declared they were " three persons and one soul." He conveyed them back to Nether Stowey in the Quantock Hills; and in that most lovely country they made their next home.

For the first fortnight they were the guests of Coleridge and his Sara, with one-year-old Hartley, in their tiny cottage. Two days after them arrived Charles Lamb, still under the shadow of tragedy,[1] the beginning of another friendship. The host himself was sadly incapacitated from taking part in those first summer walks over the hills, for, " the second day after Wordsworth came to me, dear Sara accidentally emptied a skillet of boiling milk over my foot," and, confined to " the lime-tree bower, my prison," he made the best possible compensation by imagining their pleasure in a charming poem. Their delight was equal to his expectations. " There is everything here," wrote Dorothy ; " sea, woods wild as fancy ever painted, brooks clear and pebbly as in Cumberland, villages so romantic ; and William and I, in a wander by ourselves, found out a sequestered waterfall in a dell formed by steep hills covered with full-grown timber trees. The woods are as fine as those at Lowther, and the country more romantic; it has the character of the less grand parts of the neighbourhood of the Lakes."

The dell was Holford Glen in the big woody estate that surrounds the Queen Anne mansion, Alfoxden. Such was their delight in the place

---

[1] One cannot fail to be struck by the extraordinary prevalence in the circle of insanity (both Lambs, Charles Lloyd, Dorothy, both Southeys, Lovell) and of that other pathological condition expressed in " opium-eating " (Coleridge, Burnet, De Quincey) ; and also by the undemonstrative manner of its expression as contrasted with the violent heroic insanity of the Continent in the next century (Dostoevsky, Strindberg, Van Gogh).

that they at once pictured themselves as resident in some neighbouring cottage, but hardly more than a week later the house itself became their home. They rented it furnished, at £23 a year, through the interest of Thomas Poole. This was the great-hearted tanner of Stowey who had brought Coleridge himself to the place, and whose eager philanthropy won him the friendship of the most famous men of the day. It is one of the most gracious gifts which men of genius have to bestow that they carry along with them into their own immortality the figures of their friends. The name of Thomas Poole endures; nor is it forgotten that his kindness was equally the servant of men who were less than himself as of men who were greater. Over his native hills, through the summer, winter, spring of that momentous year, wandered the great " Prophets of Nature " whom he had brought there, taking from the time and place an inspiration for the plan of their lives. It is related in *The Prelude* how almost as soon as Wordsworth accepted his poetic destiny he projected a great work in the epic tradition; but, like Milton, he was long in choosing his subject, and ranged through all possibilities in history or myth vainly seeking his proper theme. He fell into such perplexity over it, and grew so weary at the everlasting postponement of choice in spite of his conscious talent, that at last he cried out that it would have been better to have thrown himself into life itself " and ask no record of the hours " than following this poetry

to live
Thus baffled by a mind that every hour

And at that all his memories, right back to murmuring Derwent, would come surging upon him and demand of the false steward the repayment of his talents. His profound wish was to give the broadest possible account of humanity in some " philosophic song," and, with Milton as his model, he assumed the desirability of presenting it in the form of some mythological or historical narrative. But any fixed narrative appeared to confine him too much ; and Coleridge, more experienced in abstractions, provided the solution – that he should present his subject naked of formal story in the most general possible way, taking for his limitless theme " Nature and Man." This great work was to be in three parts, the whole to be known as *The Recluse*, and much of Wordsworth's thought was given to it in these days, and some parts of it written, including probably the splendid " Prospectus " which stands before *The Excursion*.

Meanwhile other matters were in hand. The November walk which William, Dorothy, and Coleridge took to visit the Valley of Rocks at Linton is now a household story ; how, to defray the expenses of their journey, they planned a poem together to be written for the *New Monthly Magazine*, and how out of their joint store of dreams, reading, and invention, *The Ancient Mariner* was evolved. The practical issues of collaboration brought to light the fundamental difference in their mental operations, and, after Wordsworth had left the Mariner to Coleridge, the proposal was made to compose a volume of poems, each working in his own manner. In Coleridge's poems " the incidents and agents were

to be, in part at least, supernatural ; and the
excellence aimed at was to consist in the interesting of the affections by the dramatic truth of such
emotions, as would naturally accompany such
situations, supposing them real." For Wordsworth's part, " subjects were to be chosen from
ordinary life ; the characters and incidents were
to be such as will be found in every village and its
vicinity, where there is a meditative and feeling
mind to seek after them, or to notice them when
they present themselves."

Now it is clear that Wordsworth regarded the
method of Coleridge with disfavour not merely
because it indicated a mental attitude widely
divergent from his own, but because it seemed to
him to be a step backward from the position
which they, as the most vital and modern minds of
the day, had attained. An essential act in their
prophetic destiny was the absolute rejection of all
the machinery of myths and symbols which
previous ages, with a more confused terminology,
had found it necessary to employ. The world of
man should be allowed to speak in its own natural
language. The whole idea of a *medium* at all was
so entirely unsatisfactory that he felt his way into
his own confused theories by which he thought to
argue away the conception of a special poetic
language. These theories arise out of the obscure
and uncomprehended feeling that a world whose
appeal to man was so immediate did not demand
an approach from him less direct than his actual
life upon it ; and yet that the indirect approach of
poetry provided another kind of delight which
must consequently somehow or other be explained.
(Hence the attempt to identify poetry with the

Ew

language really used by men ; a compromise, but the nearest he could get to identifying poetry and life.) The explanation was never really found, but in the course of his search Wordsworth fell upon so many general truths that his Preface to the *Lyrical Ballads* (2nd Ed., 1800) became one of the most valuable contributions to the study. A letter to James Tobin of March 6th, 1798, refers to essays which he is planning ; which suggests that the theory of poetry grew together with the poems themselves, not as afterthoughts to justify them, as is often stated.

Wordsworth spent the spring conscientiously composing the poems which were to form his contribution to the book : the lyrics on the influence of Nature, *The Thorn, Simon Lee, We are Seven, The Idiot Boy, Her eyes are wild.* We may note, in passing, the frequency of the theme of " Deserted Motherhood." When these passive expositions of his point of view were finished – and their beauty carries its own conviction – he set himself to compose a work which should be as nearly parallel as possible to *The Ancient Mariner* in the meaning of its story and in the final impression aimed at, but obtaining these effects through a natural instead of a supernatural means. He began *Peter Bell* on April 20th, but withheld it from publication for twenty-one years until he might have rendered it " fit for filling *permanently* a station, however humble, in the Literature of our Country." He then dedicated the poem to Southey, as being a noted exponent of the opposite view, to demonstrate that there was nothing narrowly exclusive in the position he had taken ;

a very graceful work in the genre, *The Egyptian Maid*, as though to demonstrate to a certain type of unintelligent critic that he also could do the thing perfectly well if he chose). In the dedicatory letter he writes that the poem " was composed under a belief that the Imagination not only does not require for its exercise the intervention of supernatural agency, but that, though such agency be excluded, the faculty may be called forth as imperiously and for kindred results of pleasure, by incidents within the compass of poetic probability, in the humblest departments of daily life." Beethoven, who was born in the same year as Wordsworth, expressed the same opinion in choosing an opera libretto. " As to the question of magic, I must admit that I am prejudiced against that sort of thing, because it so often demands that both emotion and intellect shall be put to sleep." Many years before, Ben Jonson had foreshadowed the prologue of *Peter Bell* when he excused the absence of monsters from *Bartholomew Fair*, saying that " he is loth to make nature afraid in his plays, like those that beget tales, tempests and such like drolleries, to mix his head with other men's heels."

On April 20th, " The Moon crescent," says Dorothy's *Journal*, " *Peter Bell* begun." Pacing, as was his wont, the gravel-path in front of the house, he took characteristically enough the vehicle for his satirical-magic journey from the moon before his eyes. He imagines himself borne by a little boat, " in shape a very crescent-moon," all over the heavens and the realms of faery. A fanciful dialogue follows between the Boat and the Poet, in which the former tries to

enthral him in the stars and planets ; but his
attention wanders back to the " dear green
Earth " and all her beauties,

> And see the town where I was born !
> Around those happy fields we span
> In boyish gambols ;—I was lost
> Where I have been, but on this coast
> I feel I am a man.

The Boat reproaches him, and lures him forth
again into more-than earthly-worlds, all in vain.

> Temptation lurks among your words ;
> But, while these pleasures you're pursuing
> Without impediment or let,
> No wonder if you quite forget
> What on the Earth is doing. . . .

> Long have I loved what I behold,
> The night that calms, the day that cheers ;
> The common growth of mother-earth
> Suffices me – her tears, her mirth,
> Her humblest mirth and tears.

So he comes down again to his own garden, where
his friends are waiting to hear from him the tale
of Peter Bell. Precisely as *The Ancient Mariner*, this
tells of the wanton cruelty of a man towards an
animal, of the consequences of that action, and
of the release of the man from the consequences
through a sudden gush of pity. But while in *The
Ancient Mariner* the consequences are magical
(vengeance by the tutelary spirits of the region for
the death of the Albatross) Peter Bell's whole mental process is a strictly psychological one. His state
of mind acts and reacts against various natural
appearances – tricks of moonlight, the echoes of
the ass's bray on the rocks, the cry of the boy

searching for his dead father, the withered leaf that follows him, details that work up a sense of freezing horror at least equal to Coleridge's and by far less obvious means. Wordsworth had deliberately chosen a much harder way of writing effectively, and it was not made easier for him that he considered it necessary from time to time to recall to his reader how his method differed from the usual one.

> Dread Spirits ! to confound the meek
> Why wander from your course so far,
> Disordering colour, form, and stature !
> — Let good men feel the soul of nature,
> And see things as they are.

" As they are " ; and yet the whole trouble with Peter Bell was that

> A primrose by a river's brim
> A yellow primrose was to him,
> And it was nothing more.

This is no mere confusion of terminology, but the passages, occurring as they do in one poem, illustrate Wordsworth's personal perplexity. We know how in his childhood he would lose himself in the external world so utterly that " I had to push against something that resisted, to be sure there was anything outside of me." This childish metaphorical instinct of seeing things, and oneself, pretendingly, in the likeness of other things instead of as themselves, did not diminish as he grew up, but grew stronger. Thus he became a poet, and one peculiarly endowed with exactness and felicity of imagery. " Nor am I naked in external things, forms, images," he writes in the self-examination at the beginning of *The Prelude*.

But this metaphorical power ran violently counter to his profounder instinct that the real world, naked of imagery, was ultimately more poetic if only it could be reached. Wordsworth's thought is Shakespearean. It is the experience of King Lear, who can only find the reality he seeks in a naked beggar. "Here's three on us are sophisticated. Thou art the thing itself." Lear's last acceptance of the consequences of that truth is to

> take upon us the mystery of things
> As if we were God's spies,

which foreshadows Wordsworth at Tintern.

In this conception of a poetry beyond metaphor we come back to his struggle to identify the poet with ordinary men. The poet is "a Man speaking to Men"; and when he added "a man, it is true, endowed with more lively sensibility," he implied simply that the poet was one who realised, like Lear, that for any man to establish communication with any other man, he must fight his way back through sophisticated imagery to "the thing itself." Thus in the poem of *The Daisy*, after "playing with similes" through several stanzas in which he tries comparing the flower with one thing after another, he ends:

> Bright *Flower* ! for by that name at last,
> When all my reveries are past,
> I call thee, and to that cleave fast.

In all this we can see the real force of the phrase "a return to Nature." For Wordsworth it was more than the reaction of an age to predecessors; it was an experience which must be lived again and again for ever in the heart of every man. It is one aspect of that conflict between the sensual and the ascetic (or, indeed, the same thing in different terms), which is observable in almost everything of permanent significance in poetry ; and tending as it does, by reason of its own nature, to question the need of, or deny the identity of, poetry at all, it has given rise to a body of criticism which has hardly yet provided the explanation which it seeks.

Wordsworth and Coleridge did not differ in creed ; but it seemed to Wordsworth that, by refusing to adopt the proper æsthetic of the creed, Coleridge had refused half its implications. The personal experience to be won from it was lost to him. Ultimately Coleridge's was a broader, but a less profound, point of view. He knew that not every man is a Lear, and that the human mind will never weary of finding entertainment in the magical. For him Nature did not exclude Super-Nature. That was a scientific, not a poetic, opposition. Every activity of which the whole man was capable had its place in poetry, all seeing, believing and imagining. (The difference in practice between them was really due to nothing more than a difference in talents. Coleridge's sensibility was more acute in one direction, Wordsworth's in the other.) The validity of the subject depended on the truth and value of the emotional responses aroused in the reader. It could therefore be accepted as real. Wordsworth, on the other hand, could find no reality in Super-Nature (and indeed Coleridge's spirit-world is not even consistent with itself). It was only a symbol for something real, and symbols, by increasing the indirectness of art, were undesirable. His own

later " loss of vision " was a falling-back into
metaphor from the life beyond metaphor, resulting
in an unwillingness to write poetry at all, and a
tendency to incorporate symbols into his style
which was new to him.

Coleridge had taken as much as Wordsworth
from the Gothic writers, and kept more. He
realised, from his criticisms of Mrs. Radcliffe, that
the supernatural event must be in itself spiritually
significant to be fit stuff for poetry, and the reac-
tions of the character towards it such as accord
with the real behaviour of men. But his æsthetic
itself remained Gothic, and that, as Wordsworth
had foreseen, involved a fatal defect in his treatment of Nature. He confused religious issues with
æsthetic. For him Nature is the Temple of God,
he the priest who would " build an altar in the
fields " – and thus become the father of nineteenth-
century hymnology. The noisy *Hymn before
Sunrise in the Vale of Chamouni* (which he had never
visited) recalls the manner of the Hebrew psalmist
singing that " the Heavens declare the glory of
God and the firmament showeth his handiwork."
Wordsworth has advanced a whole stage further
in thought, and looking down at the lilies of the
field, or the primrose by the river's brim, he says
that, even as they are, " not Solomon in all his
glory was arrayed like one of these."

The four spring lyrics which he wrote at
Alfoxden form a little sequence in themselves
epitomising his faith. With the lightest strokes
he makes infinite suggestions. The *Lines written
in Early Spring* emphasise the joy in Nature, a joy
which is only to be won back for man who has
lost it by his return to Nature.

To her fair works did Nature link
The human Soul that through me ran ;
And much it grieved my heart to think
What man has made of man.

To My Sister[1] develops the idea of a linked soul in
Nature and man, and introduces the doctrine
that Nature is a more powerful educative force
than reason or book-learning – a doctrine developed in its turn in the dialogues with Matthew
the Schoolmaster, *Expostulation and Reply*, and
The Tables Turned. The poems are clearly intended to be slightly extravagant, and Matthew,
defining books in one vivid phrase – " The spirit
breath'd from dead men to their kind " – provides a case as unanswerable logically as William's
reply :

The eye—it cannot choose but see,
We cannot bid the ear be still ;
Our bodies feel, where'er they be,
Against or with our will.

Nor less I deem that there are Powers
Which of themselves our minds impress ;
That we can feed this mind of ours
In a wise passiveness.

.   .   .   .   .

[1] In which the lines –

" No joyless forms shall regulate
Our living calendar :
We from to-day, my Friend, will date
The opening of the year," –

are the most outspoken (albeit somewhat indirect) declaration
made by Wordsworth against Christian forms. His proposal
seems to derive from the State religion of the French Republic.
This was certainly the latest, perhaps the only, date at which he
would have spoken so plainly.

One impulse from a vernal wood
May teach you more of man,
Of moral evil and of good,
Than all the sages can.

Sweet is the lore which Nature brings ;
Our meddling intellect
Mis-shapes the beauteous forms of things : —
We murder to dissect.

Enough of Science and of Art ;
Close up those barren leaves ;
Come forth, and bring with you a heart
That watches and receives.

Attempts are often made to refute these statements
of Wordsworth's by the easy sophistry of a *reductio
ad absurdum*, but it is as often forgotten how he
himself has provided for all contingencies. In
Peter Bell he makes a careful distinction between
a savage nature and the nature to which the hero
returns. He speaks of "the unshaped half-
human thoughts which solitary Nature feeds,"
and writes :

Though Nature could not touch his heart
By lovely forms, and silent weather,
And tender sounds, yet you might see
At once that Peter Bell and she
Had often been together.

A savage wildness round him hung
As of a dweller out of doors ;
In his whole figure and his mien
A savage character was seen
Of mountains and of dreary moors.

While the conversion is wrought thus-:

And now is Peter taught to feel
That man's heart is a holy thing ;
And Nature, through a world of death,
Breathes into him a second breath,
More searching than the breath of spring.

The poem *Ruth*, which was written the following
year in Germany, contrasts still more clearly two
kinds of natural influence. Ruth is a motherless
child, left to herself ; a youth who has spent a
wild life among the American Indians woos her,
weds her, and deserts her at the church door to
return to his wildness. Wordsworth attributes
his behaviour solely to the influence of Nature.

The wind, the tempest roaring high,
The tumult of a tropic sky,
Might well be dangerous food
For him, a Youth to whom was given
So much of earth – so much of heaven,
And such impetuous blood.

Whatever in those climes he found
Irregular in sight or sound
Did to his mind impart
A kindred impulse, seemed allied
To his own powers, and justified
The workings of his heart.

Nor less, to feed voluptuous thought,
The beauteous forms of nature wrought,
Fair trees and gorgeous flowers ;
The breezes their own languor lent ;
The stars had feelings, which they sent
Into those favoured bowers.

After the tragedy, he expresses the matter still
less mistakably :

> The engines of her pain, the tools
> That shaped her sorrow, rocks and pools,
> And airs that gently stir
> The vernal leaves – she loved them still ;
> Nor ever taxed them with the ill
> Which had been done to her.

The first of the stanzas quoted might be a description of Wordsworth himself. It indicates how deeply he had felt the danger that lay in himself as a lover of Nature ; while the poem as a whole is written with the special design of showing that the action of Nature depends on circumstance. The most favourable circumstances were to be found in the " humble and rustic life " which he had observed in his own country ; and – arguing again from observation, and the strictest logic – among persons of undeveloped intellect, children, and idiots. (Shakespeare again supports him. His point of view regarding madness seems to be identical ; while on more than one occasion he uses his clowns to develop the kind of suggestive paradox which is contained in Wordsworth's sayings about " humble and rustic life.") In his long letter of 1802 to Wilson defending the *Idiot Boy*, Wordsworth wrote, " I have often applied to idiots, in my own mind, that sublime expression of Scripture, that *their life is hidden with God*. " The close observation of insanity which he was destined so tragically to suffer never shook his faith. In 1838 he wrote of the imbecile Mrs. Southey :

> Like Children, She is privileged to hold
> Divine communion.

So the Alfoxden year passed in work so exhausting that it often left Wordsworth prostrate with illness. All his life long he was a victim to sick headaches, especially if he ventured into stuffy public rooms, theatres, or halls, and a like sickness would often attack him after the labour of composition. There was little of outward event during the year more than the meetings on the hills between Stowey and Alfoxden. At Christmas they spent three weeks in London, hoping to get *The Borderers* produced – in vain. In May they made one of their further excursions, to Cheddar ; and a little later Hazlitt paid his famous visit. His description of Wordsworth in the *First Acquaintance* is generally taken to be the most convincing.

There was something of a roll, a lounge in his gait, not unlike his own Peter Bell. There was a severe, worn pressure of thought about his temples, a fire in his eye (as if he saw something in objects more than the outward appearance), an intense high narrow forehead, a Roman nose, cheeks furrowed by strong purpose and feeling, and a convulsive inclination to laughter about the mouth, a good deal at variance with the solemn, stately expression of the rest of his face.

A visit of more consequence was the one paid by John Thelwall, shortly after their arrival the summer before. This noble and active Jacobin, who had just been tried for high treason, makes an interesting contrast with the poets, his activity deriving from that unswerving devotion to one idea, by virtue of which he was himself no poet. Yet he paid in his kind a tribute to the glen as

moving as theirs. "Citizen John," said Coleridge
to him, "this is a fine place to talk treason in !"
"Nay ! Citizen Samuel," replied he, "it is rather
a place to make a man forget that there is any
necessity for treason."

The memory of such a necessity, however, was
brought back to them by nothing more forcibly
than the action of the Government itself. As
early as '94 Poole had incurred its notice, and
now the behaviour of his friends, and their day-
and-night wanderings indicating some peculiar
interest in the locality, suggested the conclusion
that Alfoxden had been taken for the purpose of
planning a French invasion. The idea itself, and
the spy who was sent to observe them, are merely
comic relief.[1] But Lady St. Aubyn, the owner of
Alfoxden, heard of the matter, and not even
Poole's protest that her tenants had an uncle who
was a Canon of Windsor withheld her from letting
it over their heads. There followed, in consequence, one more year of wanderings before
they found their final home.

On June 25th, 1798, they left Alfoxden ; and
after a week with Coleridge in Stowey they went
on to Bristol, for the *Lyrical Ballads* were finished,
and Cottle had them in the press. A week was
spent working with him, and then William took
Dorothy away from the city and brought her over
the Severn ferry to the Wye. He came once more
to Tintern, and in the tranquillity of a sycamore's
shade the emotion of his whole life's joy in Nature
came rushing in upon him. His mind travelled

---

[1] See "Wordsworth, Coleridge, and the Spy," by A. J. Eagle-
ston, in *Coleridge : Studies by Several Hands* (Constable) ; and cf.
Lawrence in Cornwall, 1917.

back, past that five-years-gone day of ecstasy to
the still further days of the laughing schoolboy
time, and brought back from every moment
memories crowding up to their height of joy in
the present stillness of his mind. For the present
moment is the sum of all past moments. The last
and most personal of the theories in the *Lyrical
Ballads* Preface is that

poetry is the spontaneous overflow of powerful feelings : it takes its origin from emotion recollected in
tranquillity : the emotion is contemplated till, by
a species of reaction, the tranquillity gradually dis-
appears, and an emotion, kindred to that which was
before the subject of contemplation, is gradually produced, and does itself actually exist in the mind.

It is sometimes said that the poem of Tintern,
composed as it was entirely on the day of its conception, forms, like the opening of *The Prelude*, an
exception to his usual practice. It is rather the
supreme example of it. For the moment itself
was the tranquillity, and the emotion was his
whole recollected life, gathered up alive into the
moment. And two facts gave it an added strength
– that it, in its turn, held " life and food for future
years " – an emotion *anticipated* in tranquillity ;
and that his " dearest friend " was with him, his
sister, whose joy was still, and would remain, an
ecstasy that did not need to make comparisons ;
for

wise as Women are

When genial circumstance hath favor'd them,
She welcom'd what was given, and craved no more.
Whatever scene was present to her eyes,

So he offered up to the beauty of Wye and Tintern that thanksgiving for what he owed them which is one of the profoundest utterances ever made by man.

> Nor less, I trust,
> To them I may have owed another gift,
> Of aspect more sublime ; that blessed mood,
> In which the burthen of the mystery,
> In which the heavy and the weary weight
> Of all this unimaginable world,
> Is lightened : – that serene and blessed mood
> In which the affections gently lead us on, –
> Until, the breath of this corporeal frame
> And even the motion of our human blood
> Almost suspended, we are laid asleep
> In body, and become a living soul ;
> While with an eye made quiet by the power
> Of harmony, and the deep power of joy,
> We see into the life of things.

"I knew a man," said St. Paul – and we cannot doubt that, like the boy known to Winander, the speaker spoke of himself –

"I knew a man . . . (whether in the body, I cannot tell ; or whether out of the body, I cannot tell : God knoweth ;) such an one caught up to the third heaven. . . . How that he was caught up into paradise, and heard unspeakable words, which it is not lawful for a man to utter."

Even so, and yet articulate, was Wordsworth caught up at Tintern, a living spirit, into the vision of the life of things.

CHAPTER IV

1798–1799

THE poem, which William wrote down, whole and finished, that same night when they returned to Bristol, was added to those already in the press, and finally appeared at the end of the volume. They spent the weeks of waiting, before that momentous event, in the village of Shirehampton, near enough to watch the book's progress, but free of the hot town. Coleridge sometimes visited them there, and together they made another " dash into Wales " to visit Thelwall on " Liswyn farm " near Brecon. A plan, which had been long under discussion, of visiting Germany to learn the language and study " natural history," was now concluded, and by the end of August they were all in London making preparations. Evidently the *Lyrical Ballads* were not actually published before they left. When they did appear they " are laughed at and disliked by all with very few excepted," wrote Mrs. Coleridge, but for once her bluntness does not seem to be combined with its usual devastating apprehension of the facts. At any rate there were four editions of the book (added to in the meantime) by 1805; while a healthy symptom that its purposes might one day be achieved was the early appearance of would-be imitators. The versatile

Fw   81

Mrs. Robinson, for example, was quickly off the
mark, and in 1800 Longmans, who had published
the *Ballads* for Cottle in London, produced her
Lyrical Tales, a circumstance which nearly induced Wordsworth to change his title in subsequent editions. The volume provides ludicrous
enough examples of the use of a particular manner
without the slightest understanding of the reasons
for it, and must take some of the blame for the
persistent failure of the general public to listen
with sympathy to Wordsworth himself.[1]

The party for Germany consisted of William,
Dorothy, Coleridge, and a Stowey friend, John
Chester. They sailed from Yarmouth on Sunday,
September 16th, and two days later reached the
mouth of the Elbe. That day they proceeded as
far as Cuxhaven, where they cast anchor, and on
the following day reached Hamburg. Dorothy's
Journal, and Coleridge's *Satyrane's Letters* are both
fascinating accounts of travel and life abroad.
The charm of Dorothy's lies as usual in the
minuteness and directness of her observation.
Others may have observed as much – none was
ever endowed with so patient an imagination for
seeing the value in a detail. Coleridge was a little
too much amused with the fun of his own ideas
about things to record them for their own sakes.
Wordsworth's own contribution to the record is
too often forgotten, forming as it does a transcrip-
tion by Coleridge into the last of the letters. It is

[1] An odd coincidence is just worth recording. The hero and
heroine of a fantastic piece of nonsense in Mrs. Robinson's book
bear the names William and Annetta. But even the most
hopeful could hardly discover any further connection in the
tale, which seems to derive its action from the last scene of *The
Merry Wives of Windsor*.

a record of notes made by him of conversations with Klopstock, the venerable father of German letters, to whom they had been introduced by his brother, a rich merchant. It is clear from these notes not only that Wordsworth was very well acquainted with German literature, but that he was rather more familiar with the works of Schiller than Klopstock himself, while his judgments were in general much more accurate.

Parts of the conversation turned upon matters of special concern :

. . . I answered, that I thought the story [of Wieland's *Oberon*] began to flag about the seventh or eighth book ; and observed, that it was unworthy of a man of genius to make the interest of a long poem turn entirely upon animal gratification. He seemed at first disposed to excuse this by saying, that there are different subjects for poetry, and that poets are not willing to be restricted in their choice. I answered, that I thought the *passion* of love as well suited to the purposes of poetry as any other passion ; but that it was a cheap way of pleasing to fix the attention of the reader through a long poem on the mere *appetite*. Well ! but, said he, you see, that such poems please everybody. I answered, that it was the province of a great poet to raise people up to his own level, not to descend to theirs. . . . He seemed to think that no language could be so far formed as that it might not be enriched by idioms borrowed from another tongue. I said this was a very dangerous practice.

Klopstock's dogmatic criticism of Milton's versification, and his listeners' subsequent discovery that he had only read Milton in a prose translation at the age of fourteen, are well known.

At the beginning of October the friends separated ; Coleridge and Chester left for Ratzeburg, and William and Dorothy, with no discoverable reason,[1] made for Goslar, on the edge of the Harz. Communication was kept up as far as possible between the friends, and they exchanged copies of their latest poems, Wordsworth's including the great " Skating " passage from *The Prelude*, and that of the " Stolen Boat." Coleridge, who was very melancholy, wrote to them –

William, my head and my heart ! Dear William and
      dear Dorothea !
You have all in each other ; but I am lonely and
      want you ! –

evidently fresh from reading Goethe's *Hermann und Dorothea*, which had appeared the year before. It suggests the romantic light in which he saw the friendship of the brother and sister. At Goslar they were more dependent upon one another than they had ever been, for intercourse with such social life as the town had to offer was closed to them by their own inability to entertain, and the descent of the coldest winter known for a hundred years prevented them from leaving. Few books were accessible, and the result was a period of great activity in composition.

The war between England and France had made a great cleft in Wordsworth's patriotic allegiances which had never yet been reformulated. The rise of Napoleon and the French invasions of Holland and Switzerland put an end

---

[1] Klopstock's birthplace was Quedlinburg, not far from Goslar, and his family originated from Ratzeburg. Possibly both suggestions came from him.

to whatever kind memories he still held of France ;
and by the time of his visit to Germany his love of
England was ready to re-establish itself. Once
more he received the confirmation of a faith
through a contrast, which was heightened by what
Alfoxden had given him.

> I travelled among unknown men,
> In lands beyond the sea ;
> Nor, England ! did I know till then
> What love I bore to thee.

Henceforward patriotism was to be the foundation
for him of every kind of belief. He could find no
virtue in the consistency or constancy of ideas for
their own sake if they did not also conform with
what seemed to him a profounder and more
important instinct than the devotion to abstract
ideals – namely, the love of his country, which
was the direct expression of his love of Nature.

The " Lucy " poems were written at Goslar.
The essential fact that " Lucy " was English, dis-
poses of any possible connection with Annette.
Professor Harper makes the suggestion that the
" Dove " refers not to Dovedale in the Peak, but
to the Dovedale which leads into Patterdale above
Brother's Water ; that Wordsworth passed that
way in his first summer vacation between Hawkshead and Penrith, and fell in love with a small girl
living at the only house in the neighbourhood,
Hartsop Hall, and that she died young. There is
no evidence whatever to support this, though it
may just be worth noticing that in the *Guide to the
Lakes* Wordsworth does go a little out of his way
in a rapid survey to mention the place as " never
explored by travellers," and refers to Hartsop

Hall more than once. On the other hand, Dovedale in the Peak is mentioned in a confusing passage of *The Prelude* (VI., 208) relating to walks there and in the Lakes in his second vacation, with which both Dorothy and Mary may possibly be associated.

In the Glow-worm poem " Lucy " is definitely Dorothy, but Wordsworth never used names consistently (" Emma " has three or four different identities). Doubtless the name came to him from " Lucy Gray," the little girl whose story Dorothy had told him at Goslar, and out of which he made a small masterpiece. Coleridge thought of " A slumber did my spirit seal " that, in " some gloomier moment he had fancied the moment in which his sister might die." It is at least certain that the subject of the poem was not necessarily dead. The opening of the sequence,[1] " Strange fits of passion," describes an anxiety-fantasy that his beloved *might* be dead ; the remainder are a natural development of this into the fantasy that she was dead.

Professor Garrod, in a most illuminating discussion of the subject, half suggests, and at once rejects, the idea that the name " Dove " was chosen simply as a pleasant rhyme for " Love." But need the idea be rejected ? (After all, Coleridge invented the name " Lewti " to rhyme with " Beauty.") The point is of no great importance, and the remainder of his essay explores the heart of the matter to its furthest depths. In the analysis of a character who was so much a part of Nature that death wrought no

[1] If such they can be called. Wordsworth separated the poems in his final arrangement.

change – " dying, she is gathered up into her own world " – we seem to catch an echo of Wordsworth himself, both the child who had to grasp at an object to recall himself to reality, and the man at Tintern

> laid asleep
> In body and become a living soul.

As a writer Wordsworth's tendency was always autobiographical. (A logical conclusion of his rejection of myths and symbols would have been the total rejection of all kinds of fiction.) Equally, as a writer he must have realised the danger of confining himself to that manner. It looks as if in the " Lucy " poems he was making a deliberate attempt to carry his art a step further by abstracting his feelings about love, women, and Nature from incidents personal to himself, and presenting them in the terms of fiction. Such a step would seem to be an essential one in the career of any significant artist. While therefore acknowledging what Mary and Dorothy contributed far back to the making of Lucy, the identification of her with either of them is unnecessary. It is relevant to recall how in the period immediately preceding this he had written several fictions that describe a forsaken mother.

As soon as the winter began to break up they planned their departure from Goslar, and by the end of February were at Nordhausen, having walked right across the Harz forest. Their wanderings lasted another two months, but nothing is known of them until the end of April when they spent some days with Coleridge at Göttingen.

Early in May they were in England again, and
" right glad " to be so, wrote William, " for we
have learned to know its value."

One impulse drew them both northward, and
they made at once for Mary at Sockburn-on-Tees,
where her brother Tom had a farm. Their future
was without any plan. In October, Coleridge,
who had been making the first of his extraordinary
disappearances out of the lives of friends most
eager to help him, reappeared (he had been in
England since June, vainly sought after), and had
no sooner perceived William's love for Mary than
he conceived that passion for her sister Sara
which was at once the most hopeful and disinte-
grating affection of his life. William had been ill,
but now he and Coleridge, with William's sailor-
brother John, set off on a walking-tour in the
Lakes. He was in the country of his childhood
again ; and a certainty descended on him that
they would be separated no more. He recalled
the day on which, a " roving schoolboy," he had
broken over the hills from Hawkshead and seen
Grasmere for the first time ; how he had dreamt
of life and death there in that perfect solitude, and
how the place remained

> As beautiful to thought, as it had been
> When present to the bodily sense.

The empty future became full of the knowledge
of it as a real presence again for ever, for he found
the very cottage of Dorothy's dream. He returned
to Sockburn to fetch her ; and, as the long cold
century drew at last to its end, they began that
wild winter journey, pacing together,

Through bursts of sunshine and through flying
    showers,

over the bleak hills, while the wind

          drove us onward as two ships at sea,
    Or, like two birds, companions in mid-air,
    Parted and reunited by the blast ;

but their souls drew " a feeling of their strength "
from the stern countenance of Nature, and when

          the naked trees,
  The icy brooks, as on we passed, appeared
  To question us, "Whence come ye? to what end?"

their answer was as certain as their course – by
Wensley, Garsdale, Sedberg, Kendal, and on – in
those last bitter days " after we were left to ourselves, and had turned our whole hearts to Grasmere as a home in which we were to rest."

CHAPTER V

1800–1807

Grasmere – Dorothy's journal and William's poems – visiting Annette and Caroline in Calais – sonnets – Napoleon consul for life – new ideas – domestic wisdom – marriage to Mary Hutchinson – *To the Cuckoo* and the *Immortality* Ode – first sense of "loss" – compensation of memory – death of John – the "new control" – *The Happy Warrior* – Coleridge's illness and absence – reading of *The Prelude* at Coleorton.

So there they settled ; and, in that ideal republic of earth-proud " statesmen," Wordsworth found the permanent soil for his growth which he had learnt in Germany was his principal need. In their cottage at Town-end – formerly an inn called the Dove and Olive Branch, which only later came to be known as Dove Cottage – and especially in the garden which he made up the steep fells behind the house, he enjoyed the untouched solitude he had looked for and yet retained the advantage of belonging to a small and humble, but admirable, society. Dorothy, still more than himself, won with her irresistible charm a frank and easy intimacy with the people of the village and the roads, and the journals which she wrote, of beauty unequalled in their kind, are as moving in their descriptions of the life of the place as in the revelation of her own mind. The unclouded happiness of the Alfoxden days was a little changed now, when her passion for William grew beyond her understanding, and her love of Coleridge brought her nothing but distress. In the world about her she sought the strength to make her turbulent heart still, and she

put what she learnt from it into haunting phrases.
. . . " Grasmere very solemn in the last glimpse
of twilight. It calls home the heart to quietness."

William sought that strength, too, in his own
uncomprehended need. He was slowly coming
to recognise himself as a man who must suffer
the human destiny more intensely than others in
order that it might find speech through him.
Neither in the accidents of his past nor in the
conduct of the world towards him need the
causes of his agony be sought, but simply in his
character as a poet.

> I thought of Chatterton, the marvellous Boy,
> The sleepless Soul that perished in his pride ;
> Of Him who walked in glory and in joy
> Following his plough, along the mountain-side :
> By our own spirits are we deified :
> We Poets in our youth begin in gladness ;
> But thereof come in the end despondency and
>   madness.

The great poems written in the first years at
Grasmere – *Resolution and Independence*, *Michael*,
The Brothers – show him striving to learn bravery
from the simple endurance of rustic figures – the
shepherds and the leech-gatherer – an admiration which paved the way to his mystic joy in the
Happy Warrior. In these moving narratives his
feeling for the essential magnificence of humanity
is revealed in such clarity that the barest statement of circumstance and action achieves a poetry
that no art could adorn :

> Do thou thy part ;
> I will do mine. – I will begin again
> With many tasks that were resigned to thee :
> Up to the heights, and in among the storms,

> Will I without thee go again, and do
> All works which I was wont to do alone,
> Before I knew thy face.

To the early days in Dove Cottage also belong his most charming poems of flowers, birds, and butterflies, in some of which, for all their devoted simpleness, the art of the greatest word-painters and lyric musicians is outdone in felicity.

All this time visits and communications between Dove Cottage and Sockburn had been frequent, though no formal engagement between William and Mary seems to have been made. It is self-evident that neither of them was willing to undertake any obligation before the opinion of Annette on the matter could be clearly ascertained. In October 1801 the preliminaries of peace with France were opened. During the last three months of the year the Hutchinsons were at Grasmere. In February and March correspondence was passing between William and Annette. On May 25th the Treaty of Amiens was signed ; while in June any decision they may have come to was assisted by the news that Lord Lonsdale had died, and that his heir was at long last to repay the family debt. On July 9th William and Dorothy set out for Sockburn, spending a week upon the way, and, after ten days with the Hutchinsons, they left for London. In the early morning of the last day of July they crossed Westminster Bridge on the way to Dover, and seldom has poetry expressed so profound and utter a stillness of heart as the sonnet which he composed there, or that other one written as he walked upon Calais beach, with his daughter, one night in the following month. One might guess that there was little to disturb him; and only one conclusion can be drawn from the fact that Annette, whom he had not seen for ten years, and their daughter Caroline, whom he was seeing for the first time, came to meet him in Calais, and that they proceeded no further – namely, that her own mind was fixed before ever they met. Somehow, during the troublous times, she had earned the reputation of widowhood, and she was anxious to avoid any risk of losing it. She remained the "Widow Williams" until her death in 1841. After all, there was only one point of sympathy between them now – their loathing of Napoleon – and even that only accentuated their differences; for she had gone through fire in the royal cause, and he still wept for liberty when he remembered the Calais of his first arrival so long before with Robert Jones. On August 15th Napoleon was made consul for life; and the main outcome of this French visit was not so much the personal matter which prompted it (though the knowledge that Annette granted him his freedom and that Mary was waiting for him was doubtless the foundation for his mood) as the impulse it gave him by a new contact with reality to write those sonnets which are among the most splendid pieces in our patriotic literature.

> I have bent my way
> To the sea-coast, noting that each man frames
> His business as he likes. Far other show
> My youth here witnessed, in a prouder time;
> The senselessness of joy was then sublime!
> Happy is he, who, caring not for Pope,
> Consul, or King, can sound himself to know
> The destiny of Man, and live in hope.

In fact he had finally learnt that the destiny of man could be carried out not through the names of offices and accidental authority, but through the single hearts of men led by the enduring prophecy of such genius as Milton's, or even his own. He was in a country of enemies; and, looking back from Calais at the " fair star of evening " stooping over England, he felt more deeply for his country than ever before. With just so much sorrow and fear they looked back to the French coast from Dover, at the end of the month, rejoicing with fresh simplicity in English soil.

> Thou art free,
> My Country ! and 'tis joy enough and pride
> For one hour's perfect bliss, to tread the grass
> Of England once again, and·hear and see,
> With such a dear Companion at my side.

During the three weeks that followed in London – where there was a reunion of the whole family among other things, and Lamb took them to Bartholomew Fair – Wordsworth's feelings seem to have developed very rapidly. The " one hour's perfect bliss " changed into distress at the country's corruption, and at life lived careless of its real worth, but " only drest for show."

> Plain living and high thinking are no more :
> The homely beauty of the good old cause
> Is gone ; our peace, our fearful innocence,
> And pure religion breathing household laws.

He uttered the great summons to Milton :

> We are selfish men ;
> Oh ! raise us up, return to us again ;
> And give us manners, virtue, freedom, power.

Thy soul was like a Star, and dwelt apart ;
Thou hadst a voice whose sound was like the sea :
Pure as the naked heavens, majestic, free,
So didst thou travel on life's common way,
In cheerful godliness ; and yet thy heart
The lowliest duties on herself did lay.

Wordsworth had made a whole step further in
human experience since Tintern. There he
rejoiced in a vision that through the power of
Nature " the dreary intercourse of daily life "
could never prevail against him. He had learnt
now that it is just that intercourse which is the
whole stuff of life, and that the highest wisdom
is to accept it, and live in it fully.

Wisdom doth live with children round her knees :
Books, leisure, perfect freedom, and the talk
Man holds with week-day man in the hourly walk
Of the mind's business : these are the degrees
By which true Sway doth mount ; this is the stalk
True Power doth grow on ; and her rights are these.

In this mood he married, on October 4th,
Mary Hutchinson, and no woman could have
been more fitted to assist him in the preservation
of it. It was a mood that accepted the common
world of daily life in all its implications,
believing this to be a more true and honest
method of dealing with it than the ordinary
method of poetic escape. The way was thus prepared for his submission to the control of " Duty "
two years later, an event that led on, in its turn,
to a still more realistic attitude to life which was
demanded of him in the tragic death of his
brother. This present mood of domestic wisdom
was the logical conclusion of his belief that there

was no difference between the language of poetry and the speech of real life, that there was no real difference between the poet and other men, and that the proper subject of poetry was the humblest aspect of life. It is therefore to be noted that, while the autumn of 1802 saw a significant development in his human experience, the event constituted no change in, but rather a confirmation of, his poetic faith.

It is fair to associate this event with his so-called " loss of vision," but it would be rash to assert which was the cause and which the effect. For one thing, what Wordsworth meant by the loss seems to differ a good deal from what his critics often mean. His own first notice of it dates back to at least five years before any noticeable difference in the quality of his poetry occurs, and indeed his discussion of the loss resulted in some of his most imaginative writing.

In the " Matthew " poems (*The Fountain*, and the *Two April Mornings*), written in Germany, which develop the personality of the old schoolmaster created at Alfoxden, Wordsworth foresees, but incompletely, the kind of loss which old age might believe itself to have suffered looking back to youth.[1] In the March of 1802 he seems to have felt for the first time that he had suffered some such loss himself. Within three consecutive days he composed *To the Cuckoo*, the opening stanzas of the *Immortality* Ode, and *My Heart Leaps Up*. To the cuckoo (who seems

[1] Matthew, a " composite picture," is given the age seventy-two ; but we know that the man who contributed most to making him was William Taylor, and that Wordsworth was present at his bedside when he died, aged thirty-two – exactly Wordsworth's age in the months under discussion.

to have been the prompting occasion of all the sensations described), he says :

> Thou bringest unto me a tale
> Of visionary hours.

And of the world of Nature which surrounds him, the same always and yet different, he asks :

> Whither is fled the visionary gleam ?
> Where is it now, the glory and the dream ?

Now each of these poems, positing at the outset an actual loss, provides its own answer. There is, after all, no real loss, he says ; so long as the cuckoo sings it will always be possible to recollect the freshness of childhood in tranquillity –

> And I can listen to thee yet ;
> Can lie upon the plain
> And listen, till I do beget
> That golden time again.

> O blessèd Bird ! The earth we pace
> Again appears to be
> An unsubstantial, faery place ;
> That is fit home for Thee !

—while the last stanza of the Ode does not really seem to contrast his present condition with his past one more distinctly, or recognise a more fundamental difference than that which he made between the visits to Tintern of 1798 and 1793. Any difference is to be found only in the new sadness of expression, when he says that

Though nothing can bring back the hour
Of splendour in the grass, of glory in the flower . . .
  Gw

I love the Brooks which down their channels fret,
Even more than when I tripped lightly as they ;
The innocent brightness of a new-born Day
            Is lovely yet ;
The Clouds that gather round the setting sun
Do take a sober colouring from an eye
That hath kept watch o'er man's mortality ;
Another race hath been, and other palms are won.
Thanks to the human heart by which we live,
Thanks to its tenderness, its joys, and fears,
To me the meanest flower that blows can give
Thoughts that do often lie too deep for tears.

Already at the beginning of the Ode we learn
that the matter of it had been not a fixed condition, but a passing mood, and that " a timely
utterance gave that thought relief " – the " Rain-
bow " poem, namely, in which he declares his
faith in the continuity of human experience.

> The Child is Father of the Man ;
> And I could wish my days to be
> Bound each to each by natural piety.

The matter, therefore, is simply the fear of losing
the sense of his own continuity, which was precisely
the problem facing him now in his preparation for
writing *The Prelude*. It is notoriously difficult in
surveying one's past to believe in the identity of
the central figure in such spectral scenes with one's
living self. He speaks of this difficulty himself
more than once in *The Prelude*. It is a reasonable
supposition that brooding over his past for the
sake of *The Prelude*, as he had been doing in
Germany, ended in this analytical and questioning
mood as a result of which the composition of the
poem hung fire until the beginning of 1804 ; when
the quietness which Mary brought him, and his

new kind of acceptance, allowed the work to be taken up again.

Wordsworth's " loss of vision " is scarcely more, then, than the overwhelming consciousness that he was no longer a child. At that time he suffered exceptionally what all children suffer in greater or less degree – the helpless inability to save himself from self-loss in the external world. " At that time I was afraid of such processes," he said, and he would adopt Johnsonian methods to recall himself. As late as the age of twenty-eight, or twenty-nine (at Tintern, and dramatically in " Lucy ") he could still lose himself in this way, but now gratefully and without fear, and the transport of self-loss was greater in proportion as the self to be lost was weightier with

> The burthen of my own unnatural self,
> The heavy weight of many a weary day.

It is self-evident that, unless he were deliberately to arrest his growth at this point, the burthen must eventually become too heavy for such transports of self-loss to continue. He refused the alternative, allowed the burden of manhood to increase, and forwent the advantages of escape into a child-condition. Continuing the note above cited he says : " In later periods of life I have deplored, as we have all reason to do, a subjugation of an opposite character." But, as he adds, what he never lost was the memory of those transports –

> O joy ! that in our embers
> Is something that doth live,
> That nature yet remembers
> What was so fugitive !

> The thought of our past years in me doth breed
> Perpetual benediction . . .

The faculty of memory which (except in the
matter of dates, understandably enough in so long
a life) he possessed in unique degree, owing to
intense impressionability in the moment of experience, was always able to provide him with that
sense of continuity which he valued so highly.
For no matter what sorrows befell him, the present
was the sum of all the past, and the past was a
procession of radiant moments whose light never
failed. Nevertheless there were occasions, natural
enough to the melancholy inherent in him, when
he would deplore the loss of the physical transport
itself, as in the poem, *Composed upon an Evening of
Extraordinary Splendour and Beauty* (1818). One has
but to compare Coleridge's *Dejection* Ode (like
Wordsworth's first laments also produced in the
spring of 1802) to realise how different a matter
such loss might be when memory could supply
nothing but bitterness.

Now the store which Wordsworth set by
memory, his belief in " the spiritual presences of
absent things," and, indeed, the whole poetic
theory of " emotion recollected in tranquillity,"
were a kind of heroic compensation in the life of
one who had learnt terribly the actual meaning of
loss. The description of himself as

> Having two natures in me, joy the one
> The other melancholy,

is abundantly evidenced from the first recorded
moments of his childhood, and many of his moods

express the normal romantic yearning, for which reasons need not be sought. The poem of the Leech Gatherer, written a little later this spring, shows how intense his agony could be in battling with reasonless fits of melancholy. Yet the story of his life up to this moment supplies almost reasons enough for them, while from now on through the half-century up to his death he was to be the sufferer from accidents requiring a tremendous strength to save his own life from destruction by them.

The central figure in this connection, and one who more than any other gave the bias to the course of Wordsworth's subsequent thought, was his younger brother John. A sailor in the merchant service, " a Poet in everything but words," he was the adored friend of everyone who knew him, and a hero for William and Dorothy, to whom he gave a love almost as great as theirs for each other. All his adventures on the high seas – and in time of war he was in constant danger – were undertaken in the thought of bringing back a fortune to share with his brother and sister. He was their first visitor at Dove Cottage, and spent from January to the September of 1802 with them, helping them arrange the rooms and plant the garden stretching up to the fells. At the end of one of his visits they walked with him some of the way over Grisdale Hawes towards Patterdale.

> Here did we stop ; and here looked round
> While each into himself descends,
> For that last thought of parting Friends
> That is not to be found.
> Hidden was Grasmere Vale from sight,
> Our home and his, his heart's delight,

His quiet heart's selected home.
But time before him melts away,
And he hath feeling of a day
Of blessedness to come.

During the December of 1804 they hoped he would be able to visit them, but he was kept south by business in connection with the ship, *Earl of Abergavenny*, command of which he had obtained through their friend Wilberforce. On February 6th, 1805, the ship struck a rock off Weymouth, and sank to the bottom. John, with nearly every other soul on board, was drowned.

William and Dorothy and Mary broke down ; for " grief will . . . and must have its course : there is no wisdom in attempting to check it." But " God keep the rest of us together ! " said William, in one of his most heart-piercing cries ; " the set is now broken." And Dorothy wrote, " I can never again have a *perfect* – that is an unchastized – joy in this world."

For two months Wordsworth wrote nothing. By May he was able to finish *The Prelude* (at which he had begun serious work at the beginning of the previous year). After that he wrote the *Elegiac Stanzas suggested by a Picture of Peele Castle in a Storm*, the memorial verses already quoted from, and the *Character of the Happy Warrior*.

These are some of his most flawless poems, and they are of great personal significance, as they make explicit at last a number of ideas which had been growing for several years, and which the shock of John's death had completed. In the first he recalls those still summer weeks he spent near Peele eleven years before, at the time of

Robespierre's death, and suggests how the whole
of life might then have been pictured for him
like that sea in perfect summer stillness, even in
the poetic unreality of " the light that never was
on sea or land."

> So once it would have been, – 'tis now no more ;
> I have submitted to a new control :
> A power is gone, which nothing can restore ;
> A deep distress hath humanised my Soul.
>
> Not for a moment could I now behold
> A smiling sea, and be what I have been :
> The feeling of my loss will ne'er be old ;
> This, which I know, I speak with mind serene.

The " new control " is evidently that of " Duty,"
a word which is made to bear in the Ode, which
was written about half a year earlier, rather more
meaning than it usually conveys ; it has perhaps
borrowed a little more than the form from Gray's
Ode to Adversity. By the death of John, Wordsworth
has learnt to accept " with mind serene " the
order of a world in which such events have their
part. This is no surrender ; it is made in the
profound belief that in the acknowledgment of
laws man achieves a richer freedom than is
possible under the constraining responsibilities of
individual liberty.

> Through no disturbance of my soul,
> Or strong compunction in me wrought,
> I supplicate for thy control ;
> But in the quietness of thought :
> Me this unchartered freedom tires ;
> I feel the weight of chance-desires :
> My hopes no more must change their name,
> I long for a repose that ever is the same.

John's death compelled him to demand peremp-
torily what his instinct had already bidden him
ask for in prayer. And it is certain that had
Wordsworth not been able to do so life could not
have been longer endured by him. It is another
example of his progressive genius for realism that
he could abandon old supports for new and
stronger ones whenever the need arose.

It is interesting to note, in passing, the resemb-
lance in the ideas and wording of this stanza to
those of the sonnet on the sonnet, " Nuns fret
not," which was possibly written at this time; and
it is symptomatic of his acceptance of the value of
an external order that he chose to make such
frequent use of the sonnet during these years.

There also now emerges, complete, an idea
which indeed is hardly concealed at any time in
Wordsworth's life. It is the familiar one that the
life of action is one to be desired and honoured
above the life of thought. Wordsworth's life
always contained so much physical activity, and
the poetic life was so much more nearly akin to the
active than to the philosophic, that he suffered no
violent reaction against poetry; though it is very
probable that the idea of a poem called *The
Recluse* became increasingly distasteful to him.
For the life and death of John stirred him deeply.

> Farewell, farewell the heart that lives alone,
>   Housed in a dream, at distance from the Kind !
> Such happiness, wherever it be known,
> Is to be pitied; for 'tis surely blind.
>
> But welcome fortitude, and patient cheer,
>   And frequent sights of what is to be borne !
> Such sights, or worse, as are before me here. —
> Not without hope we suffer and we mourn.

Finally, in the *Character of the Happy Warrior*, he made that mystic tribute to the heroic which is unsurpassed for concentration of meaning and feeling. We see at the outset in what particular point the Happy Warrior fulfilled an ideal towards which Wordsworth himself, with *The Prelude* just finished, had been labouring.

> It is the generous Spirit, who, when brought
> Among the tasks of real life, hath wrought
> Upon the plan that pleased his boyish thought.

The hero, in fact, is one who never loses the sense of his own continuity, one in whom the parts of himself are never at war with one another, because they have never been divided.

A grief less overwhelming in its finality, but with all the prolonged torments of uncertainty, was the sickness of Coleridge. When they came to Dove Cottage he settled at Greta Hall, Keswick, and during the next three years the journeys between Grasmere and Keswick, and the prolonged visits made at each other's houses, were to be the only – but memorable and picturesque – incidents in their lives. Coleridge's unfortunate domestic circumstances, and the gradual breakdown of his health, filled William and Dorothy with constant anxiety. In August 1803 they started on a tour of Scotland together, but Coleridge's nervous condition prevented him continuing after a fortnight. William and Dorothy went on alone, and did not return till nearly the end of September. They had meanwhile met Scott for the first time at Lasswade ; and collected a mass of impressions, to be turned by Dorothy into her *Recollections of a Tour in Scotland*, and by William into a number of his most imaginative lyrics, including the various tributes to Burns, *To a Highland Girl*, *The Solitary Reaper*, *Stepping West-ward*, and *Yarrow Unvisited* – singular examples of a chance scene, figure, or phrase realised so over-whelmingly as " a fact " of beauty that they haunt him for ever afterwards with accumulated meaning.

Coleridge meanwhile decided that some warmer clime was essential for his health; he was taken ill at Grasmere that December, on the way to London, when Dorothy and Mary nursed him, and, after endless delays, departed for Malta in April 1804. As soon as he was gone, Wordsworth settled down to *The Prelude*, which was being written as a special gift for him, that it might be ready against his return.

It was nearly three years before they saw him again, and for most of that time they were without any tidings of him whatever. Holidays were post-poned, plans made and cancelled, in response to rumours that reached them, for their anxiety was not to be away from Grasmere at the time of his arrival. Every item of news from the war brought with it the extra fear that he might be in danger. Yet the death of John, whose value he had been among the first to discern, elicited no word. A little more than a year after his departure, *The Prelude* was finished and waiting for him ; and at every season he was expected, and still he never came. At last it was impossible for them to put off any longer their project of spending some time at the farmhouse at Coleorton, lent to them by their friend Sir George Beaumont, and there eventually, in January 1807, to a changed

Coleridge, took place the long-awaited recitation of the poem on the Growth of a Poet's Mind.

When, in 1798, there was first evolved the plan of a great philosophic work to be called *The Recluse, or Views of Man, Nature, and Society*, the actual distribution of the parts was rather left to arrange itself during the progress of the composition, for "I know not anything which will not come within the scope of my plan." But the more he pondered on the subject of mankind in the abstract the more often he was driven back to test the truth of an idea in himself; and he was convinced that before undertaking the work he must make a "rigorous inquisition" of himself to see how far the life he had lived fitted him for it. He therefore wrote this poem, ultimately to form an introduction to the major work, but addressed in the beginning privately to Coleridge, and without the intention of publishing it during his lifetime. For, as he wrote to Beaumont, he knew that it was

a thing unprecedented in literary history that a man should talk so much about himself. It is not self-conceit, as you well know, that has induced me to do this, but real humility; I began the work because I was unprepared to treat any more arduous subject, and diffident of my own powers. Here, at least, I hoped that to a certain degree I should be sure of succeeding, as I had nothing to do but describe what I had felt and thought; therefore could not easily be bewildered. This might certainly have been done in narrower compass by a man of more address, but I have done my best.

From time to time during the remainder of his life Wordsworth worked over the poem until it reached the form in which it was published after his death. The publication of both texts by Professor de Selincourt, with full *apparatus criticus* and an acute introduction, has removed as far as possible the shadows of a later time from the first impressions. The later text shows on the whole fewer and less fundamental modifications of expression towards orthodoxy than had been anticipated, while it is remarkable for consistent improvement in style,[1] frequent enrichment of poetic expression, more concentration, and more clarity of meaning.

Wordsworth has had less than justice done to the actual quality of his writing, because, setting less store by it than most poets for its own sake, he tends to draw deliberate attention to the inadequacy of words as a medium in order to stress the value which he sets by the matter itself – the interesting result being that the words themselves occasionally obtrude over the meaning, having been provoked, so to speak, into flaunting their inadequacy. (In his later writing, where the meaning derives less directly from the weight of his own experience, and more from story and symbol, the words are more elaborately cared for.) There can, however, be no excuse for failing to meet Wordsworth on his own terms. " True it is," he remarks himself, with customary realism, " Qui *bene* distinguit bene *docet* ; yet fastidiousness is a wretched travelling companion ; and the best guide to which, in matters of taste, we can entrust ourselves, is a disposition

---

[1] To the many points observed by Professor de Selincourt may be added the frequent change of double negatives into simple positives, e.g. " type not false " becomes " true epitome."

to be pleased." Small profit can accrue from bringing a kind of sophisticated criticism into places where its terms are not admitted ; and it is better to accept Wordsworth whole.

With *The Prelude*, however, these questions scarcely arise. It is one of the richest possessions of the English language, not only for the weight of its matter, but equally for the beauty of its language. In passage after passage every rift is loaded with ore; few poems can show such a frequency, none, perhaps, such absolute felicity and exactitude in the choice of imagery for metaphor and simile. Wordsworth is with Milton the great master of the prolonged classical simile in English, and the ceaseless variety of picture, the constant entertainment of the mind with remote comparisons, is one among the great charms of *The Prelude*. This marks an advance in his technique over the barer narrative of *Michael*, and a step towards his later style; but, as the images are invariably natural ones, they are still consistent with that craving for immediacy which lies behind the *Lyrical Ballad* theories. Moreover the images perform to an unusual degree the function of adding to a statement by exhibiting it in a new light, and with a precision which is unsurpassed. It may be said that the matter of *The Prelude* could not be completely recounted in one word less than its actual number.

Coleridge listened rapt ; and in his sad address to Wordsworth, written after the recitation, caught something of his old life out of the memories which the poem had stirred. But, during those days at Coleorton, William and Dorothy found to their unspeakable sorrow that their former friend had vanished beyond recall. Sickness and weakness and misfortune had irreparably damaged all contacts between him and other men. Yet they still hoped, and still gave their uttermost to help him.

> A well of love – it may be deep –
> I trust it is, – and never dry :
> What matter ? if the waters sleep
> In silence and obscurity.
> – Such change, and at the very door
> Of my fond heart, hath made me poor.

CHAPTER VI

1808–1815

Wordsworth's children – move to Allan Bank – estrangement from Coleridge – at the Rectory – move to Rydal Mount – tract on the Convention of Cintra – *The Excursion* – Wordsworth's conflict – *The White Doe of Rylstone.*

WORDSWORTH's first son, John, was born in 1803, and a year later came the daughter Dora, who was to fill so vital a part of his affections in later years. In 1806 a second son, Thomas, was born, by which time Dove Cottage had long ceased to provide adequate accommodation for its regular inhabitants, still less for the constant stream of visitors – De Quincey, the Coleridges, and the Hutchinsons – who would sometimes spend months together there. In June 1808, shortly after their return to Grasmere from Coleorton, they moved out of Dove Cottage into Allan Bank, a large new house with commanding views of the lake and valley, where, in September, a second daughter, Catherine, was born. Before the end of that month Coleridge, by now the victim of an elaborate persecution-complex, had joined them. In the previous February news that he had broken down in London reached Wordsworth, who hurried up to Town, and devoted a month to the thankless task of trying to help him. Since then correspondence had passed which proved to them that Coleridge was no longer normally responsible for what he wrote; but, still persisting in the attempt to save what was still their most treasured friendship, they exposed themselves to bitter criticism for his sake. For it was clear to them that nothing so much was wanting as the courage finally to separate from his wife, and, though aware of the contumely they would bring upon themselves, they took the new house largely with the object of giving him a separate home.

Life at Allan Bank was chaotic, for there was no increase of income to meet the expense of their larger quarters. *The White Doe of Rylstone* was finished, but, in spite of the good reasons urged by Dorothy, William refused to consider its publication. Through the demands of necessity some kind of journalism was contemplated. Meanwhile, during the last months of the year, Coleridge mused over his plans for *The Friend*, and Wordsworth was hard at work over his great Tract on the Convention of Cintra. The Tract was published in May 1809. *The Friend* appeared at last in June, and continued fitfully till the following March. Sara Hutchinson, who set herself to bear the combined strain of being loved and tormented, took down nearly the whole work at Coleridge's dictation, and when she departed, broken in health, there was little hope of its continuing. In May 1810 Coleridge returned to his wife at Keswick, in order to be out of the way when Mary gave birth to a third son, William. He passed by Allan Bank in October, on the way to London with the Montagus ; and a few days later his mania for self-laceration reached its tragic climax in seizing on a provoked piece of tactlessness by Montagu to justify that breach with Wordsworth to which he had been driving ever since the return from Malta. It was nearly

six months – and after they had moved from Allan
Bank into the old rectory opposite the church –
before the Wordsworths discovered what had
happened. After another year of miserable perplexity and despair over the reports that reached
them, William was unable to endure it any
longer, and in May 1812 went up to London,
where at last, through the mediation of their good
friend Crabb Robinson, a reconciliation was
effected. But the passionate intimacy of early
years was gone beyond recall.

While he was still in Town little Catherine
suddenly died in her fourth year; and in
December Thomas, who was six, contracted
measles and followed her. These successions of
grief did much to age Wordsworth and darken
his mind. The immediate result was their
determination to leave the unhealthily situated
rectory where two such unhappy years had been
passed. In March 1813 their financial anxieties
were relieved by William's obtaining, through
Lord Lonsdale, the office of Distributor of Stamps
for Westmorland, through which they might
reckon on an increase to their income of about
£400 a year. And on the first of May took place
their removal to Rydal Mount, which was to
remain their home till the end of their lives.

During these restless and afflicted years Wordsworth had continued to work at *The Excursion.*
There can be no doubt that some of the unsatisfac-
toriness in the scheme of the poem and the lack
of definition in its object are due to the circumstances in which it was composed. Wordsworth's
intentions with regard to it certainly changed

Hw

considerably from what they had been at the time
of its original conception. The best part of eighteen years had elapsed before he concluded the
work in 1814, and no creative mind can remain
fixed during so long a period, least of all one open
to adapt itself to new conditions as his was.

Besides, these years had also seen much other
composition, including the whole of *The Prelude*.
As soon as he had managed to complete this, a few
months after the death of John, he turned himself
to the expression of that new attitude into which
the virtue of his humanity had been consistently
developing, and to which John's death had given
a sudden tragic confirmation. Most of the second
part of the Poems Dedicated to National Independence and Liberty was written in the next
years (1807–11) and form poetic examples of the
enthusiasm which prompted the Tract on the
Convention of Cintra. This great and enduring
work was occasioned by the shameful signing at
Cintra on August 30th, 1808, of the convention
under which the British deliverers of Spain
handed back to the French, whom they had
defeated at Vimiera, the advantage which they
had won there. In deploring this betrayal of the
principles of liberty Wordsworth, as he constantly
asserts in contradiction of a statement made in
Parliament, was voicing the unanimous opinion of
the people. He also happened to find himself in
agreement with the Tories – an accident which
was to occur with increasing frequency in subsequent years. But it cannot be too strenuously
emphasised that Wordsworth at no time underwent any kind of revolution in himself. What he
suffered was the torment of having to account to

himself for his own consistency in face of a
constantly changing world. Realist that he was,
he was willing to accept new terms in politics,
more definite forms in belief (and, as a corollary,
more regular symbolism in his poetry) ; but the
principles remained to be defended. " You have
been deluded by *Places* and *Persons*," he once
wrote of the kind of critic to whom the word
" France " still meant something which was out of
date by twenty-five years, " while I have stuck to
Principles." Thus in the Tract he explains how
men such as himself who had in the beginning
most bitterly opposed the war, were now the most
willing to pursue it.

Their conduct was herein consistent : they proved
that they kept their eyes steadily fixed upon principles ; for, though there was a shifting or transfer
of hostility in their minds as far as regarded persons,
they only combated the same enemy opposed to them
under a different shape ; and that enemy was the
spirit of selfish tyranny and lawless ambition.

And again,

in order that we may have steady PRINCIPLES to con-
troul and direct us, (without which we may do much
harm, and can do no good,) we ought to make it a
duty to revive in the memory those words and facts,
which first carried the conviction to our hearts :
that, as far as it is possible, we may see as we then
saw, and feel as we then felt.

Few political writers have been more emancipated
in their awareness that " the relations of things to
each other are perpetually changing." And it is
remarkable that even after he had come to
accept, through John's death, a " new control "

outside himself, he allowed no relief to the responsibility of the individual in action, when

Principle is indispensably requisite. I mean that fixed and habitual principle, which implies the absence of all selfish anticipations, whether of hope or fear, and the inward disavowal of any tribunal higher and more dreaded than the mind's own judgment upon its own act.

Such is the splendid and powerful language in which the Tract is written. (A rather too frequent indulgence of the long sentence is apt to make the reading difficult.) Wordsworth's sound and well-informed exposition of Nationalism is of great interest to the historian; to the biographer it is another aspect of the patriotism which for many years had been fundamental in all parts of his activity. More remarkable is the exultant strain in which he reaffirms his faith in the principles of Liberty and Democracy. This occasion called from him a far more ringing and thrilled declaration of that faith than ever the French Revolution had done. There are passages in which he is carried rapt with enthusiasm into just such a mystic state as he had entered at Tintern. It is significant that the finest of these is the one which concludes his prophecy that Liberty would have delivered Spain, not evidently from Catholicism as such, but from the peculiar bigotry and primitive superstition which it manifested in that country, to a more reasonable and thoughtful faith; for

the domestic loves and sanctities . . . wherever they have flowed with a pure and placid stream, do instantly, under the same influence, put forth their strength as in a flood ; and, without being sullied or polluted, pursue – exultingly and with song – a course which leads the contemplative reason to the ocean of eternal love.

But more significant, in a sense, than anything it contains is the fact that he wrote it at all. Wordsworth never took any active part in politics. "Launch thy bark," he wrote,

On the distempered flood of public life,
And cause for most rare triumph will be thine
If, spite of keenest eye and steadiest hand,
The stream, that bears thee forward, prove not, soon
Of late, a perilous master.

His association with the Kendal election of 1818 was very largely due to his friendship with the Lowther family, and has received a little more publicity than the occasion demands from the chance that Keats happened to call at Rydal Mount while he was away. As a poet, of course, there could be no bounds to the subjects in which he might interest himself. Yet the fire of his thought and expression in the Tract is largely due to that passionate admiration of action and the new value which he had learnt to see in it through John. In this light the Tract is a complement to *The Excursion*; they are evidently products of the same mood. He makes a striking reference in the passage on Spanish Catholicism to the " domineering imagination, by which from childhood . . . the human creature . . . has been betrayed, and the debasing affections which it has imposed in him "; and the whole working of the poetic faculty seemed to him to become less and less trustworthy. As we have seen, the balance of interests in Wordsworth was at all times so unusually well adjusted that no violent reaction could ever have taken place; but it is undeniable that John's life and death did incline him to put greater faith in the kind of life he had lived. Wordsworth refused to reject any part of life whatever – any kind of activity for which any kind of man might feel a need ; yet his conscience could penetrate the implications of all such activities. In the possession of this imagination which at once comprehends the realities of the whole human world and transcends it, he resembles Tolstoi.[1] He remained a poet to the end of his life because he realised that in that capacity he was ultimately most effective ; but he could sometimes hardly disguise the longing to have been a participator in actions whose results were more immediately visible, and the occasional bitterness which appeared at one period in his old age may reasonably be traced to this.

In fact he had joined the Volunteers at Ambleside, on his return from the Scotch Tour of 1803, when the fears of an invasion were at their height. He writes in the Tract, five years later : " These are times . . . when the character and duties of a soldier ought to be understood by every one who values his liberty " ; and when he declares that " many of the Volunteers " would have offered

---

[1] There are obvious resemblances in particulars, e.g. their reading of history. Wordsworth writes in the Tract : " The dominion, which this Enemy of mankind [Napoleon] holds, has neither been acquired nor is sustained by endowments of intellect which are rarely bestowed, or by uncommon accumulations of knowledge ; but it has risen from circumstances over which he had no influence." This is exactly the point of view in *War and Peace*. Wordsworth's instinctive opinions on parliamentary representation were Tolstoi's mature ones (cf. *Tolstoi*, by Gerald Abraham, in this series, pp. 125-6).

their services in the Peninsula he is clearly
speaking for himself. The writing of the Tract
provided him with an opportunity of satisfying
his need, vicariously, but with such complete
demands upon his passion that the whole of his
identity could be surrendered to it. The analysis
of that identity in division of itself formed the
matter of *The Excursion.*

Much of the difficulty in arriving at any clear
conception of what the whole poem of *The Recluse*
was to be lies in the question of the identity of the
Recluse himself, and what character he was to
present. It appears from the Preface, written in
1814, that the Recluse was to be the poet himself,
the first and third parts of it consisting " chiefly
of meditations in the Author's own person." It
received its title " as having for its principal
subject the sensations and opinions of a poet living
in retirement." *The Prelude* (some of whose matter
must certainly have once been intended for *The
Recluse*) does not describe a retiring kind of
character. In the first book of the first part of
The Recluse (the only book of the first or third parts
to be written) he manages to get his poet, who is
himself, together with his sister, into retirement ;
but that is as far as the matter went. It is surely
clear that the reason why the work was never
finished was simply that the whole idea of retirement and seclusion had become thoroughly alien
to him. He had passed the time when such an
idea (in any case originally put forward by
Coleridge) was sufficiently congenial to be adopted
as the framework of a philosophical poem. And
the perhaps unexpected way in which *The
Excursion* developed as composition proceeded

made the rest of the work virtually impossible ;
for the dramatic discussion of seclusion, which is
one of the main themes of that poem, and the
close inspection to which the Solitary is subjected,
leave little opportunity for a Recluse (who is
presumably the " I " of *The Excursion*) to take
up any impressive station as the central figure of
two other whole parts. Moreover, this Solitary
in *The Excursion* is more than once called the
Recluse himself. Was there to be a Recluse
within a Recluse, so to speak ? The confusion
would have required the most careful handling.
√ True, Wordsworth, writing in 1814, still looks
forward to the completion of the whole, and
explains that the middle part has got finished first
as being " designed to refer more to passing events,
and to an existing state of things " ; but we need
not give too much consideration to Wordsworth's
public account of his works. There is little need,
for example, to pursue his identification of the
protagonists in *The Excursion* with various public
figures, or of the Happy Warrior with Nelson.
His object in making these identifications is
perfectly clear. He was aware that the peculiarly
personal character of his poetry was liable to
minimise the extent and universality of its appeal,
and it occurred to him that the attachment to
public names would assist his readers to re-create
by association its personal significance in their
own lives. Doubtless he took certain suggestions
from the sources he names. We know that
Nelson's death moved him deeply ; but the
inspiration of the Happy Warrior was his
private hero, John. And unquestionably the
actors of *The Excursion*, as all critics from Hazlitt

onwards have realised, are each of them Wordsworth himself.

This at least is true of the Wanderer and the
Solitary, who are living dramatic characters.
The Pastor is hardly more than a narrator of
other people's lives, while the " I " merely serves
to bring Wordsworth in as a mouthpiece for the
whole. We are just aware that he is a Poet, one
who has come upon the scene to "record in
verse " these arguments. But the character of
being a Poet – as one is a Wanderer, another
a Solitary – typically enough does not seem worth
his bringing into the discussion at all. It might
perhaps have been reserved for treatment in the
other parts of *The Recluse*, but the whole force of
the Wanderer and the Solitary lies in their dramatic presentation as opposites facing one another.

The character of the Wanderer was sketched
by 1798, and finished during the winter 1801–2,
two years after the substance of the first two books
of *The Prelude* had been composed. The persons
described in both places are essentially identical,
the Wanderer being built up out of precisely the
same effects of natural education as Wordsworth
was. One feels that it is mere chance that the
result in one case was this Wanderer, in the other
a Poet. And Wordsworth confesses as much.
Wandering, he says, was his passion ; and in this
man he represented " an idea of what I fancied
my own character might have become in the
circumstances."

The Solitary is equally a projection of himself.
If the Wanderer stands for that active and happy
life to which he enviously aspired, the Solitary is
the conflicting frustrated part of himself in extreme

consciousness of failure to attain the life of John. As with the Wanderer, an autobiographical fact is provided to account for his present mental condition : the Solitary, like Wordsworth, had given his faith to the French Revolution. It is remarkable that this Recluse is not presented as a Poet.

Each of these characters represents fantasies about himself, as he might become, or might have been, had the whole of either predominated. They are at the same time descriptions of himself, as he was ; for he was constantly aware that he had a joyful and a melancholy nature united in him, and these are the two natures personified. He wrote the poem for his own benefit, to prove to himself the possibility of resolving the conflict. Whether he succeeded or not hardly matters ; but at least he did achieve some kind of an adjustment with the world which made his continuance in it, in spite of past bitterness, possible and even happy. The heroic mastery with which he preserved his passions through the long years of old age is extremely impressive ; and it would be a singular judgment which could not concede some tolerance to the small human failings which testify how much he still was of a man. It will be more apt to recall Alexander Grosart's judgment : " The closer one gets to the man," he writes, " the greater he proves, the truer, the simpler ; and it is a benediction to the race, amid so many fragmentary and jagged and imperfect lives, to have one so rounded and completed, so august and so genuine."

In urging the possibility of correcting Despondency, which is the connecting thought of *The*

Excursion, Wordsworth inclines to force his point at the expense of his material. All the stories which get told in the course of the narrative to illustrate this truth – the tales told by the Pastor of the dead which lie in the churchyard, even the *Ruined Cottage*, rewritten as it was in a tone far different from its original – all of them suffer, charming and vivid as they are, from having been shaped to a special purpose. *Michael* was a story in which he was so absorbed for its own sake that poetry and truth grew out of its sheer realisation as a fact. But in *The Excursion* Wordsworth's tendency is to be more interested in the idea exemplified by the story than in the story itself. This is a perfectly reasonable and natural development in the method of a poet who was so eager to see the immediate effects of his teaching that he was tempted to abandon poetry for an active life. The glory of *The Excursion* lies in other parts of it – those splendid speeches in which the characters of the Wanderer and the Solitary wrestle with one another. All the agony of Wordsworth's natural melancholy, his self-doubtings, and the pain of loss, find expression in the passionate addresses of the Solitary to the Wanderer.

> Stripped as I am of all the golden fruit
> Of self-esteem, and by the cutting blasts
> Of self-reproach familiarly assailed ;
> Yet would I not be of such wintry bareness
> But that some leaf of your regard should hang
> Upon my naked branches.

One does not know which more to admire here, the profound psychological truth of the situation,

or the beauty and fitness of the image[1] which
expresses it. Admittedly the expression was not
always so equal to the matter, because of the
touching faith which he put in the matter to do
a poet's work without any assistance from himself.

> Life, death, eternity ! momentous themes
> Are they – and might demand a seraph's tongue,
> Were they not equal to their own support ;
> And therefore no incompetence of mine
> Could do them wrong.

This would, indeed, serve as a fair account of the
way in which a poem like *Michael* came into being.
He had absorbed the subject with such passion
that the barest telling of it was also the most
poetical. He did not realise that the more
abstract theme of a philosophical poem cannot
re-create itself with the same intensity. Nevertheless there are rich occasions when the sheer
truth of a statement arrests us into disregard of
the poverty of its dress.

> How little can be known –
> This is the wise man's sigh ; how far we err –
> This is the good man's not unfrequent pang !
> And they perhaps err least, the lowly class
> Whom a benign necessity compels
> To follow reason's least ambitious course ;
> Such do I mean who, unperplexed by doubt,
> And unincited by a wish to look
> Into high objects farther than they may,
> Pace to and fro, from morn till even-tide,
> The narrow avenue of daily toil
> For daily bread.

[1] It recalls the opening of Shakespeare's Sonnet No. lxxiii,
which Wordsworth quotes in a letter ; but tree-imagery is
frequent in his poetry, and it is well known that he took a close
and practical interest in the forestry of the Lake District.

      " Yes," buoyantly exclaimed
The pale Recluse – " praise to the sturdy plough,
And patient spade ; praise to the simple crook,
And ponderous loom – resounding while it holds
Body and mind in one captivity ;
And let the light mechanic tool be hailed
With honour ; which, encasing by the power
Of long companionship, the artist's hand,
Cuts off that hand, with all its world of nerves,
From a too busy commerce with the heart ! "

The Excursion deserves close attention not only
for the complete and accurate analysis of mental
sickness which it makes, but also for the psychological penetration that points unerringly to the
cure. With every year Wordsworth's mind gained
in the power of anticipating the interests of later
generations.

The Excursion was published in 1814 ; and the
event was signalised by the critic of the *Edinburgh
Review* achieving for himself in one fatuous phrase
the most unhappy of all literary immortalities.
Even Coleridge, to whom the poem proved something of a disappointment, was moved to an outburst. " If ever guilt lay on a writer's hand, and
if malignity, slander, hypocrisy, and self-con-
tradictory baseness can constitute guilt, I dare
openly, and openly (please God) I will, impeach
the writer of that article of it." The writer was
subsequently made a Lord, for his services, not
to literature but the law.

While *The Excursion* was being prepared for the
press Wordsworth wrote his great poem *Laodamia*,
which, he said, " cost me more trouble than
almost anything of equal length I have ever
written." It has a classic self-perfection which

allows appreciation of it to be made with less reference to the external circumstances of composition than is usual with Wordsworth's poems. At most we may note that in choosing the subject he expressed his sympathy very generally with the classical ideal of chastity, though it was not this matter which put the subject into his thoughts at all, but the growing and withering trees of sympathetic nature which, described in the last stanza, put the story into its proper focus. His alterations of the conclusion, and his desperately conscientious discussion of the problem in a letter, are the only personal evidences in the poem, and they reveal the ordinary natural conflict of any human creature – from a converted Peter Bell to a sober tutor of the classics – with his different impulses. In the first printed version (1815) he deviated entirely from the original myth by letting off the over-passionate Laodamia altogether from her punishment. In 1827 he was persuaded to doom her, in agreement with Virgil, " to wander in a grosser clime, apart from happy ghosts," for eternity ; but five years later he relented, and doomed her only " to wear out her appointed time " – thus compromising between the authority of the myth, and his own inclinations, in a way which, so far from exhibiting moral intolerance, does his heart the greatest credit.

Wordsworth wrote only one other poem from classical antiquity, *Dion*, in which the same aspiration to classic austerity is shown defeated by exposure in action.

During this summer of 1814 he made his second visit to Scotland with Mary and Sara Hutchinson. In the company of James Hogg he visited

Yarrow, and wrote the central piece, *Yarrow Visited*, in the trilogy which began with *Yarrow Unvisited* in 1803, and ended with *Yarrow Revisited* in 1831. These are among the clearest examples of Wordsworth's imaginative treatment of what is really a common human tendency. When, in 1793, with Robert Jones, he saw Mt. Blanc for the first time, he

> griev'd
> To have a soulless image on the eye
> Which had usurp'd upon a living thought
> That never more could be.

The process of anticipation was almost as important a one for him as that of recollection. In 1803 he and Dorothy refused to turn aside to see the Yarrow, saying :

> Be Yarrow stream unseen unknown !
> It must, or we shall rue it :
> We have a vision of our own ;
> Ah ! why should we undo it ?

When now he saw the true river at last, he had to work past the first disillusion and death of his fancied image till he realised that :—

> thou, that didst appear so fair
> To fond imagination,
> Dost rival in the light of day
> Her delicate creation ;

thereafter advancing in safety to the statement :

> I see – but not by sight alone,
> Loved Yarrow, have I won thee ;
> A ray of fancy still survives –
> Her sunshine plays upon thee !

which leads on to a new kind of anticipation, the one he enjoyed at Tintern and never ceased to trust :

> I know, where'er I go,
> Thy genuine image, Yarrow !
> Will dwell with me – to heighten joy,
> And cheer my mind in sorrow.

At no time did his delight in beauty lose the power of recreating its emotion at a later tranquil time and when after seventeen years the " unaltered face " of the river contrasted with his own change he wrote that its image was " dearer still to memory's shadowy moonshine." In the following spring, 1815, the *Poems in Two Volumes* containing the " Fancy and Imagination " Preface appeared ; and in May *The White Doe of Rylstone*, to which some extra work had been given since it was finished in 1807, made its long deferred appearance, and provided an early occasion for Jeffrey to confirm himself in his wretched infamy. " This," he opined, " has the merit of being the very worst poem we ever saw imprinted in a quarto volume."

The White Doe of Rylstone is Wordsworth's most flawless achievement as an artist, and stands high among the finest narrative poems in the language. Yet none of his poems has been more unduly neglected. Strictures made by Coleridge in a letter of 1808 are sometimes repeated against it ; but surely it is clear that Wordsworth revised, and perhaps reconstructed, the whole poem precisely in accordance with those criticisms during the years that lapsed before it appeared. For one thing his mention of " the delivering up of the

family by Francis " refers to nothing in the poem
as we have it now ; and the example which he
gives of, what would indeed be a " serious defect "
if it were true, " a disproportion of the Accidents
to the spiritual Incidents," is equally remote
from the facts. He says that Emily, the heroine,
" is indeed talked of, and once appears, but
neither speaks nor acts in all the first three-
quarters of the poem." Actually Emily appears
indispensably to the action in five out of the seven
cantos ; and of the two from which she is personally absent, the first introductory one comes
to its climax in the moment when the Doe sinks
down upon her grave, and the third finds its
climax in the moment when her father looks up
at the banner which she worked, and remembers
her and the Doe in dismay. One may therefore
assume that when Coleridge first saw the poem
it was more or less as he describes it, and that
accepting his just strictures Wordsworth made a
fairly complete reconstruction of it. He did this
by adopting the classical device of introducing a
narrator, the Old Man, by which Emily remains
in contact with the action personally through
almost its whole course. As the central picture
in that narrated action is the banner with which
she is inseparably associated, the result is an
exceptionally compact piece of plotting. If this
account of the matter be accepted, *The White Doe*
may pass as the work in which Coleridge's help
produced the most practical results. It is confirmed by the fact that the Old Man's sudden
appearance and attachment to the story is its
one structural weakness.

The poem was written from a motive analogous
Iw

to that which prompted *Peter Bell*. He wished
to show that narrative poetry such as Scott was
popularising in his own way could be equally or
more successful by subordinating the external
action to the spiritual meaning.

Sir Walter, [he writes] pursued the customary
and very natural course of conducting an action,
presenting various turns of fortune, to some out-
standing point on which the mind might rest as a
termination or catastrophe.

He for his part dispensed with external events for
their own sakes, employing them only in so far
as they forward the internal drama. His own
account of the manner in which externals and
internals are related is interesting :

Objects (the banner, for instance) derive their
influence, not from properties inherent in them, not
from what they *are* actually in themselves, but from
such as are *bestowed* upon them by the minds of those
who are conversant with or affected by those objects.

As an incidental result the external drama is
itself extremely moving. The moment, for
example, when Francis takes the banner from the
taunting soldier is unsurpassed in power ; and the
bare line –

He took it from the soldier's hand –

has as much weight in it as Michael's –

And never lifted up a single stone.

The story of the poem was suggested to Wordsworth by the old ballad " The Rising of the
North," and describes the ruin of the family of
the Nortons by joining in that attempt to restore

Catholicism. The father and seven of his eight
sons devote their lives to the cause. The eldest
of the sons, Francis, belongs to the new faith, as
also does the only sister Emily, who at her father's
command has nevertheless worked for him the
significant banner of the Cross which leads them
to their death. Francis makes a heroic attempt
to persuade them from the foolish undertaking,
and, having failed, receives from his doomed
father the last request to bear the banner back
to the shrine of Bolton Priory. He thus becomes
the victim of a genuine tragic conflict of divided
loyalties, and loses his life in fighting to carry out
the will of his father which is counter to his own.
Coleridge made a criticism· of some point when
he observed that the loyalties of the seven sons
and the faith of Francis and Emily were in-
sufficiently contrasted ; that something was required " in order to place the two protestant
malcontents of the family in a light that made
them beautiful as well as virtuous." It is surprising that Wordsworth did not, for reasons other
than artistic, take this opportunity of expressing
himself on a matter which he is supposed to have
felt very deeply. That he refrained is one of the
most cogent proofs of his actual tolerance in
religious matters. Had he done so the situation
might have gained in definiteness ; but he wished
to reduce external circumstance to a minimum,
and that he achieves so strong a sense of conflict
without underlining its origins is part of his art.
Moreover, Francis does not really take up his
standpoint on the ground of faith at all ; he is
merely attacking the futility of his father's attempt,
knowing as he does that nothing can result from

it but death and the extinction of the family.
The difference of faith is used only as a useful
detail. The lines from *The Borderers* which preface the poem make this clear. Action is tran-
sient ; the suffering which results is permanent,
and is the only trace which action leaves behind
it. But there is a power by which the suffering
soul may achieve peace and restoration in itself.
In the utter emptiness and ruin of fortune which
Emily remains to witness, the Doe appears, not
just as a symbol of this power, but as a reality so
suggestive that she seems to embody the very
Spirit of Nature.

For the genius and beauty of the poem lie in
the function of the Doe herself. The poem is
hers, and the story of Emily is read through the

> Endless history that lies
> In her silent Follower's eyes.

The Doe's entrance at the beginning is devised
with consummate art. It is a summer Sunday
morning late in Elizabeth's reign. Bolton's
church bells are ringing, the crowds of villagers
noisily pass through the yard on their way to
church. The service begins and an utter summer
stillness fills the yard outside.

> The only voice which you can hear
> Is the river murmuring near.
> — When soft ! — the dusky trees between,
> And down the path through the open green,
> Where is no living thing to be seen ;
> And through yon gateway, where is found,
> Beneath the arch with ivy bound,
> Free entrance to the churchyard ground —
> Comes gliding in with lovely gleam,

Comes gliding in serene and slow,
Soft and silent as a dream,
A solitary Doe !
White she is as lily of June,
And beauteous as the silver moon
When out of sight the clouds are driven
And she is left alone in heaven ;
Or like a ship some gentle day
In sunshine sailing far away,
A glittering ship, that hath the plain
Of ocean for her own domain.

She moves at her ease about the place

           until at last
Beside the ridge of a grassy grave
In quietness she lays her down ;
Gentle as a weary wave
Sinks, when the summer breeze hath died,
Against an anchored vessel's side ;
Even so, without distress, doth she
Lie down in peace, and lovingly.

There is mystery, even the sense of magic – but how different from the Gothic machinery ! – in the short quiet movements of the beast in and out of the poem, and we speculate, as the villagers do, over the strangeness of her regular Sunday appearance in the place. Wordsworth's art is sustained to the very end. Gently he adds, piece by piece, to the explanation, and never once with shock or surprise. No sudden revelation is thrown upon the mystery – it shapes itself slowly into a marvellous fact ; while the wonder of the Doe unfolds like a flower, gradually and naturally with the poem, and is only made complete in the closing lines.

This is a work which creates its own world of

legend and mood so perfectly that its personal
significance may be lost sight of. Yet it is just
the kind of poem which we might expect to
appear incidentally during the composition of *The
Excursion*; attempting to estimate by experiment
the comparative values of action and medita-
tion. In Francis, Wordsworth seems to be fighting
against his temptation to forsake poetry, and the
story of the brother and sister suggests another of
the anxiety-fantasies as to what might happen to
himself and Dorothy. His conclusion combines
the best of the methods followed by both the
Wanderer and the Solitary ; and the Doe resting
among the ruins of the Abbey expresses as a
historic truth the lesson learnt personally near the
ivy-clad stones of Tintern that Nature alone is
faithful as alone outlasting the deeds of men.

> There doth the gentle Creature lie
> With those adversities unmoved ;
> Calm spectacle, by earth and sky
> In their benignity approved !
> And aye, methinks, this hoary Pile,
> Subdued by outrage and decay,
> Looks down upon her with a smile,
> A gracious smile, that seems to say —
> " Thou, thou art not a Child of Time,
> But Daughter of the Eternal Prime ! "

So far was he from having lost the personal
knowledge of youth that he had learnt to extend
it by application to whole ages of men. If the
expression had lost something of its former
intensity it was because the field of vision was
growing continuously round him.

CHAPTER VII

1816–1850

The Eminence of Age – short period of melancholy – characteristics of later poetry – achievement of faith – natural and Christian religion – Dora – vigour of old age – Reform and Science – last tours – the Salzburg letter – Mary – the Rydal circle – fame – Poet Laureate – death. ᵥ

WORDSWORTH entered upon a long, patient, and dignified old age. In the noble discourse of the Wanderer which opens the last book of *The Excursion*, Age is spoken of as a " final EMINENCE "–

> a place of power,
> A throne, that may be likened unto his,
> Who, in some placid day of summer, looks
> Down from a mountain-top. . . .
> . . . while the gross and visible frame of things
> Relinquishes its hold upon the sense,
> Yea almost on the Mind herself, and seems
> All unsubstantialized.

Age, he continues, does not separate us from the plains below for our " utter loss," but confers

> Fresh power to commune with the invisible world,
> And hear the mighty stream of tendency. . . .

The poet, he implies, like the saint long practised in visionary striving, may at last reach through force of habit a spiritual condition in which striving gives place to tranquillity. The power of habit had been emphasised in the Preface to *Lyrical Ballads*.

For our continued influxes of feeling are modified
and directed by our thoughts, which are indeed the
representatives of all our past feelings ; and as by
contemplating the relation of these general representatives to each other, we discover what is really
important to men, so, by the repetition and continuance of this act, our feelings will be connected with
important subjects, till at length, if we be originally
possessed of much sensibility, such habits of mind will
be produced, that, by obeying blindly and mechanic-
ally the impulses of those habits we shall describe
objects, and utter sentiment, of such a nature, and
in such connexion with each other, that the understanding of the Reader must necessarily be in some
degree enlightened, and his affections strengthened
and purified.

It cannot be denied that Wordsworth came to
put a little more faith in habit than ordinary
humanity justifies. The common reader who does
not feel those impulses alive in himself may find
Wordsworth's obedience to them at times too
simply " blind " and " mechanical " – just as he
was apt to trust too simply in the virtue of his
material to provide its own poetry. But the
picture which the Wanderer gives of an elevated
old age is a true account of his own achievement.
His life of poetry was not finished. The passionate
lines *Composed upon an Evening of Extraordinary
Splendour and Beauty* in 1818 are often taken as his
conscious farewell to the visionary life, but the
patent fact that he never made any such resigna-
tion compels us to look for a less ruthless explanation. The poem describes, characteristically, the
overwhelming sensations of a moment. The mood
is profoundly tragic, one of his constitutional fits

of melancholy, brought on by a scene of sunset-romance. Just as the condition of his mind in 1802 gave rise to the opening stanzas of the *Immortality* Ode, so now the melancholy, which is frequently noticeable in a period roughly indicated by the dates 1816–20, found expression in similar utterances such as this. There were reasons enough to involve him in restlessness and depression. His elder brother, Richard, died in 1816, leaving all the family affairs in a state of appalling confusion. The same year his French daughter, Caroline, married Jean Baudouin in Paris, and the correspondence and negotiations over the marriage settlement were difficult and tedious. In 1818 friendship with Lord Lonsdale involved him in active politics, and at the end of the year, heedless of warnings from the family that his poetry would suffer for it, he became a J.P. because " I am anxious to discharge my obligations to society." More than this, he was perhaps hardly yet reconciled to the treatment with which *The Excursion* had been received, and contact with younger poets, together with the growing up of his own family, suggested to him that his own life was passing. A beautiful poem, written in September 1819, acknowledges his own autumn, and gracefully hands over his inheritance to the rising generation.

> Nor doth the example fail to cheer
> Me, conscious that my leaf is sere,
> And yellow on the bough : –
> Fall, rosy garlands, from my head !
> Ye myrtle wreaths, your fragrance shed
> Around a younger brow !

But the time of melancholy passed, and he was yet to write poems that rank among his most significant achievements.

In 1843, on the day when he declined the first offer of the Laureateship, he wrote in a letter that "no change has taken place in my manner for the last forty-five years." In view of the popular belief that some fundamental alteration in the character of his poetry took place at some date (variously placed between 1807 and 1818), it is worth noting this evidence that Wordsworth himself acknowledged such a change in the composition of the first lyrical ballads, but believed that everything which he had written since that time had been consistent. Nevertheless in half a century of work we may well expect to find some superficial changes and experiments. For a consideration of them it will be fitting to revert to the Wanderer's picture of Age looking down from the mountain-top.

What characterised Wordsworth's poetry from 1797 onwards was its immediacy – the attempt to reach a poetry beyond metaphor. The poet was a man speaking to men ; he lived un-apart in the plains of humble and rustic life. The habit of vision brought him with age up to a "final eminence "; but that separation from the plains with its loss of immediacy affected the relation of his poetry to the real world. He tends to fall back into metaphor. With almost any other poet "falling-back" would be a reverse of the appropriate expression, and even here its aptness may be questioned. But while in former times it was his genius to create poetry out of the naked statement of fact, in later years he shows a willingness to resort to the more ordinary uses of symbol, personification, and mythology. Myths came to have a particular significance for him. Coleridge had lamented that Wordsworth " was not prone enough to believe in the traditional superstitions " of the Quantocks, and, as we have just seen, the reasons which he gave then still held good. But now that he is safe from faery charms he can see in them survivals of the most elemental approach to nature, and, as such, values them, as in *The Haunted Tree* (1819) and *The Wishing-Gate* :

> . . . How forlorn, should *ye* depart
> Ye superstitions of the *heart*,
> How poor, were human life !

Nevertheless, from time to time he restates the creed which he had enunciated in *Peter Bell*. In the sonnet, " Her only pilot the soft breeze," written in about 1826, he imagines himself surrounded with various personifications, and then delightfully breaks off –

> But, Fancy and the Muse,
> Why have I crowded this small bark with you
> And others of your kind, ideal crew !
> While here sits One whose brightness owes its hues
> To flesh and blood ; no Goddess from above,
> No fleeting Spirit, but my own true love ?

Again, in the elaborate poem *On the Power of Sound*, written two or three years later, after a passage of mythology which Keats might have been proud to write, he cries :

> To life, to *life* give back thine ear :
> Ye who are longing to be rid
> Of fable, though to truth subservient, hear
> The little sprinkling of cold earth that fell
> Echoed from the coffin-lid.

Graceful personifications and a good deal of classical mythology may be found in these poems of later years. The latter interest was due to his revived reading in the classics undertaken to assist his son John in his examinations. The immediate results were *Laodamia* and *Dion*, but the influence of the classics on the style of nearly all his subsequent work is extensive and frequently happy. His characteristic fascination with sky-mythology, especially of moon and clouds, led to the writing of a great number of poems on those subjects which almost embody an individual system of his own. One of his latest poems is the lovely, *How beautiful the Queen of Night*, which comes at the end of a long series of Moon-poems mostly written during his last twenty-five years.

There was a further and more important effect of this new metaphorical attitude. He tends to use his subjects more directly as symbols of a meaning than he used to – and perhaps, also, to choose those subjects more directly for a purpose. One cannot fail, to be struck by the number of times the words " type " and " emblem " occur, translating a scene of beauty into the sphere of morals with that hurtful impatience which Lamb had noticed in *The Old Cumberland Beggar* (1797), but which was then dispensed with for many years. It derives from that eagerness that his poems should succeed in fulfilling their chosen purpose which informs so many of his letters.

> This Lawn, a carpet all alive
> With shadows flung from leaves – to strive
>   In dance, amid a press

Of sunshine, an apt emblem yields
Of Worldlings revelling in the fields
    Of strenuous idleness.

The manner is, of course, not only confined to the
later poetry. In the tremendous forms of the
Simplon Pass he had seen " the types and symbols
of Eternity " – but then the phrase is used to
clinch an accumulation of vivid images. The
comparison suffices to show that the difference is
more one of degree than of kind, and that the
effect of the use depends on the intensity of
imagination and aptitude of the comparison. In
1825 he produced one of the simplest and most
perfect symbols in all his poetry when he saw in
the skylark –

Type of the wise who soar, but never roam ;
True to the kindred points of Heaven and Home !

Symbolistic treatment goes further than the
plain use of a connecting word. In Wordsworth's
greatest poems a scene of beauty is apprehended
so passionately by the mind and senses for its
own sake that a world of wisdom grows out of
the enduring memory which the emotion leaves
behind it. As he grew older the poet came un-
consciously and naturally to value the wisdom
more profoundly than the beauty from which it
had grown. Many interesting comparisons might
be made between early and later poems illustrative
of this difference. A fair example is afforded by
the *Westminster Bridge* sonnet (1802), and one
written in 1819 on *Malham Cove*. The first is a
description of completely realised beauty, the
second, after a brief descriptive opening, continues –

Oh, had this vast theatric structure wound
With finished sweep into a perfect round,
No mightier work had gained the plausive smile
Of all-beholding Phoebus ! But, alas,
Vain earth ! false world ! Foundations must be laid
In Heaven ; for, 'mid the wreck of IS and WAS,
Things incomplete and purposes betrayed
Make sadder transits o'er thought's optic glass
Than noblest objects utterly decayed.

Clearly he has felt the scene æsthetically, but in expressing it he cannot now forbear jumping the sensation to come straight at the moral. The procedure is perfectly understandable. It can by no means be taken as regular in later composition, but it offers a fair illustration of general differences.

The later Wordsworth is a stylist of the first order. In the " melancholy " period of 1816–20 he seems to have been experimenting in the use of words for their own sake in a way not observable before, and in the process he produced a number of surprising excesses in artificial diction. With more ingenuity than sensibility he describes, for example, the playing of a church-organ in the words " the tubed engine feels the inspiring blast." That such passages are to be found at hardly any other time than these four years out of half a century of regular composition indicates their experimental nature. Thereafter his style continues consistent with his earlier principles.[1] In care and accuracy it steadily improved, and went to the making of many pieces of great art.

[1] He disclaimed these as such, however, on several occasions, e.g. in 1836 : " I never cared a straw about the ' theory ' and the ' preface ' was written at the request of Mr. Coleridge, out of sheer good nature."

In one of the earliest and still most excellent books on Wordsworth, Myers gives a good account of the earlier and later styles. "Both the simplicity of the earlier and the pomp of the later poems were almost always noble; nor is the transition from the one style to the other a perplexing or abnormal thing. For all sincere styles are congruous to one another, whether they be adorned or no, as all high natures are congruous to one another, whether in the garb of peasant or of prince." It is necessary to add that of "pomp" there is far less in the later poems than this suggests. Till the day of his death Wordsworth's prevailing interest remained with Nature and humble life, and he brought to it the simplicity which he had learnt in childhood was the only true love.

The unfading beauties of his last poems are the reaffirmation of that faith. From the exquisite sonnets on *The River Duddon* (1820) to such moving and characteristic poems as *The Widow on Windermere Side*, the two sonnets on *Furness Abbey*, and the *Love-lies-Bleeding* poems, written in the last decade of his life, he continued to assert the influence of Nature on the human mind, and the advantage which is enjoyed by those privileged to enjoy direct communion with her.

Wordsworth was a man of diversely tending thoughts and conflicting impulses to belief, but he did achieve with age the only integration of them which could have allowed his living the full length of his life. He reconciled in himself the religion of Nature and the dogma of the Anglican Church without any compromise to either. "I look abroad upon Nature," he wrote, "I think of

the best part of our species, I lean upon my
friends, and I meditate upon the Scriptures,
especially the Gospel of St. John; and my creed
rises up of itself with the ease of an exhalation,
yet a fabric of adamant."

The steps by which he reached these heights of
faith were too gradual to be distinguished; and
the experiences of his spirit had carried him so far
beyond the meaning of ordinary terms that only
the outlines of the shape of his thoughts can be
traced. His love of Nature was mystically involved with love of his country; and the love of
his country, to have any significance at all, made
certain demands upon the arrangement of his
intellectual concepts. He recognised, with his
customary realism, that the citizenship by which
he set so much store could not be considered
complete unless he professed membership of his
country's Church. The growth towards this
profession was so comprehensive and so firm that
nothing of his earlier penetration of the mystery
of things was lost by the way. The most extraordinary misconceptions exist concerning the
influence of Christianity on Wordsworth's poetry.
Of the derided Victorian piety there is hardly a
trace. The *Ecclesiastical Sonnets* (mostly written in
1821-2) which contain some magnificent poetry,
treat almost entirely of historical subjects or
Church forms. They also contain *King's College
Chapel* and *Mutability*, with its "unimaginable
touch of Time." In a letter, written in 1840, he ex-
pressly says, "I have been averse to frequent mention of the mysteries of Christian faith," and such
open didacticism as he allowed himself in his poems
is hardly ever associated with Church dogma.

It is clear that Christianity brought to him experiences as strange and transfiguring as did the beauty of Tintern, and that he did not need to make any distinction between the one and the other. In *Processions*, a poem written in recollection of a scene at Chamonix in 1820, a mystic alliance, or rather identification, of natural and Christian religions takes place which is a basis for all his subsequent belief. After a stately and imaginative reconstruction of pagan ceremony, he describes a scene which he had witnessed.

At length a Spirit more subdued and soft
Appeared – to govern Christian pageantries :
The Cross, in calm procession, borne aloft
Moved to the chant of sober litanies,
Even such, this day, came wafted to the breeze
From a long train – in hooded vestments fair
Enrapt – and winding, between Alpine trees
Spiry and dark, around their House of prayer,
Below the icy bed of bright ARGENTIERE.

Still in the vivid freshness of a dream,
The pageant haunts me as it met our eyes !
Still, with those white-robed Shapes – a living Stream,
The glacier Pillars join in solemn guise
For the same service, by mysterious ties ;
Numbers exceeding credible account
Of number, pure and silent Votaries
Issuing or issued from a wintry fount ;
The impenetrable heart of that exalted Mount !

The nearest parallel to this perfect example of " emotion recollected in tranquillity " is the far-distant poem on the *Daffodils*. Now the natural scene acting upon the mind and senses gives rise to an emotion which is not contradicted, but

Kw

confirmed and completed by the symbol of the
Cross. In the final stanza of the poem he insists
on the necessity of preserving the oneness of the
emotion experienced, and repeats his warning
against " Fable," and the pagan temptation " to
crowd the world with metamorphosis."   If
Wordsworth's life is to be divided up into defined
periods it would be far truer to take this Continental tour of 1820 as the beginning of a fresh
career than to close the book with the sunset of
1818, or earlier, as the case may be.

One other poem, a sonnet composed about 1833,
must suffice to prove how profound and genuinely
poetic an experience the Christian story gave
him. The subject is a monument by Nollekens.

> Tranquillity ! the sovereign aim wert thou
> In heathen schools of philosophic lore ;
> Heart-stricken by stern destiny of yore
> The Tragic Muse thee served with thoughtful vow ;
> And what of hope Elysium could allow
> Was fondly seized by Sculpture, to restore
> Peace to the Mourner. But when He who wore
> The crown of thorns around his bleeding brow
> Warmed our sad being with celestial light,
> *Then* Arts which still had drawn a softening grace
> From shadowy fountains of the Infinite,
> Communed with that Idea face to face :
> And move around it now as planets run,
> Each in its orbit round the central Sun.

If the intensity of poetry be not in the last par
of this sonnet, where shall it be found ? It woul
be easier to discover a parallel among the mystic
of the seventeenth century than in the pietisti
tradition of the nineteenth.

The expression of the first part of the sonnet recalls a letter written to Landor in 1824, on the subject of *Laodamia*, in which Wordsworth definitely assigns a compensatory origin to all religions. The matter is important because there is other evidence for supposing that he did not achieve his faith with that complacent ease which is generally supposed of him ; it is even likely that the case was violently contrary. Naturally he was no more demonstrative of the personal struggle in himself than he had been in the affairs of love, and he respected what he considered due from himself as a patriot and public figure. We have already noted that nearly everything which he wrote or spoke on Church matters concerned forms rather than belief. There are reasons for doubting whether he ever attained a profound and permanent faith in the future life. The possibility that he was at times tormented with doubts confirms the impression of the visionary nature of the religious experiences which he enjoyed.

He had to bear the pain of outliving not only almost all his contemporaries, but three of his own children, a grandchild, and many younger friends. When John died we find him arguing the necessity of a future life in a letter to Beaumont; and faith does not require argument and proofs. Thirty years later his beloved sister, for whom he had too rashly prophesied an age of exquisite memories, broke down in the sickness which condemned her to a quarter-century of death-in-life ; and all his dearest friends were dead. In the *Extempore Effusion* he made a glorious tribute to the memory of Coleridge,

Lamb, Scott, James Hogg, Crabbe, and Mrs. Hemans. But his grief found no kind of compensation.

> Like clouds that rake the mountain-summits,
> Or waves that own no curbing hand,
> How fast has brother followed brother,
> From sunshine to the sunless land !

" The sunless land " is hardly the language of the Hymns. A poem written to Mary in 1824 is a frank confession of doubt.

O dearer far than light and life are dear,
Full oft our human foresight I deplore ;
Trembling, through my unworthiness, with fear
That friends, by death disjoined, may meet no more !

Twenty years later he wrote in a letter :

What I lament most is that the spirituality of my nature does not expand and rise the nearer I approach the grave, as yours does, and as it fares with my beloved partner.

His honest wrestling never ceased. It appears that in quieter circumstances he won the faith he needed, and the outside world never doubted but that he enjoyed all the comforts which the Church offers. Yet when, three years before his own death, he met the most bitter agony of all his long life in the death of Dora, the intensity of his grief passed the comprehension of his most sympathetic friends.

Dora's fascination was of such a kind as seldom survives its own day, yet even now we are spellbound by the fragments of her charm surviving in letters and memories. As he watched her grow out of a wayward child into a radiant woman, Wordsworth beheld everything which he had most adored in Dorothy and Mary summed up in one creature. The whole weight of passionate love which he had felt for his wife and sister was made young again in the adoration which he gave his daughter. She had always been delicate, and, six years after her marriage to Edward Quillinan, she died, after a long illness, on July 9th, 1847. It was nearly a year before Wordsworth could control his grief. The kindly Crabb Robinson, who paid his usual Christmas visit, witnessed him break down in church on Christmas Day, and wondered at the inability " to endure an affliction imposed upon him by a power he equally loves and venerates." James, the faithful family servant, " took the liberty " of saying as much to his master. " He merely said – ' Oh she was such a bright creature ' – And then I said ' *But Sir don't you think she is brighter now than she ever was ?* ' And then Master burst into a flood of tears." " Those," says Crabb Robinson, " were not tears of unmixed grief." It is not clear what he means; but it does look as though Wordsworth's grief was mixed with fear of " the sunless land."

The living Wordsworth is never easy to keep before our eyes. The man vanishes into a voice, a vehicle of prophecy. It is all the more important to watch the signs of his passion and the long struggle with himself in which the tradition of mankind was worked out and the prophecy born. He wrestled for his beliefs in a torment more silent, but no less real, than the passion of saints.

From easy pietism he was separated by worlds of thought and pain. There is a story which at least suggests that he had achieved his full faith at last. A few days before he died, Mary stooped over his bed, and said : " William, you are going to Dora."

He made no reply at the time, and the words seemed to have passed unheeded ; indeed it was not certain that they had even been heard. More than twenty-four hours afterwards one of his nieces came into the room, and was drawing aside the curtain of his chamber, and then, as if awakening from a quiet sleep, he said, " Is that Dora ? "

He had maintained his tremendous strength and vitality until the very last. While friend after friend fell round him into insanity or death he alone remained, with nothing impaired but his eyesight, in the full vigour of youth. In his sixtieth year " he is still the crack skater on Rydal Lake," wrote Dorothy, in one of her last letters to Mary Lamb, " and, as to climbing of mountains, the hardiest and the youngest are yet hardly a match for him." And she also says, " In composition I can perceive no failure, and his imagination seems as vigorous as in youth." Posterity has not agreed with Dorothy's judgment, but it is possible to-day to see him with some of her sympathy. He brought himself over from one century into another, and still looked forward. New policies and new inventions were all acceptable to him in themselves, if they were consistent with what he deemed best for his country. His imagination invariably saw further than the men who were handling them, and comprehended their implications more clearly. He heartily

supported the principles of Reform, but opposed
what seemed to him to be a very bad Bill ; and his
attitude to education may yet receive striking
confirmation by experience. His moving prophecy regarding science and poetry is only now
being fulfilled. In the Preface of 1800 he had
written :

If the labours of Men of science should ever create
any material revolution, direct or indirect, in our
condition, and in the impressions which we habitually
receive, the Poet will sleep then no more than at
present ; he will be ready to follow the steps of the
Man of science, not only in those general indirect
effects, but he will be at his side, carrying sensation
into the midst of the objects of the science itself. The
remotest discoveries of the Chemist, the Botanist, or
Mineralogist, will be as proper objects of the Poet's
art as any upon which it can be employed, if the time
should ever come when these things shall be familiar
to us, and the relations under which they are contemplated by the followers of these respective sciences
shall be manifestly and palpably material to us as
enjoying and suffering beings. If the time should
ever come when what is now called science, thus
familiarized to men, shall be ready to put on, as it
were, a form of flesh and blood, the Poet will lend
his divine spirit to aid the transfiguration, and will
welcome the Being thus produced, as a dear and
genuine inmate of the household of man.

More than thirty years later the sincerity and
endurance of this boast were put to a harder
trial than he had foreseen, and did not fail in it.
He wrote a sonnet on *Steamboats, Viaducts, and
Railways.*

Motions and Means, on land and sea at war
With old poetic feeling, not for this
Shall ye, by Poets even, be judged amiss !
Nor shall your presence, howsoe'er it mar
The loveliness of Nature, prove a bar
To the Mind's gaining that prophetic sense
Of future change, that point of vision, whence
May be discovered what in soul ye are.
In spite of all that beauty may disown
In your harsh features, Nature doth embrace
Her lawful offspring in Man's art ; and Time,
Pleased with your triumphs o'er his brother Space,
Accepts from your bold hands the proffered crown
Of hope, and smiles on you with cheer sublime.

Nevertheless his enthusiasm for science did not destroy his discrimination of its purposes, and he fought furiously to defend the Lakes from the invasion of the railway.

The letter of Dorothy's quoted above mentions the inflammation of his eyes. Miss Batho has shown that " for the last forty years of his life he was living under the threat of blindness, that he was frequently in severe pain, and that for long periods, twice at least for more than a year at a time, he was physically incapable of reading and writing and of continuous poetic composition." It is hardly necessary to stress the effect of this, apart from other privations, upon the attempt to finish *The Recluse*. In his long last years he was dependent both for reading and writing on the willing service of Mary and Dora. Fortunately he had long ago acquired the habit of mental composition out of doors. The distress confirmed his temperamental disposition to physical activity, and " I think he walks regularly more than ever," wrote Dorothy, "finding fresh air the best bracing to his weak eyes." He also indulged in all kinds of other favourite activities, including travel. In 1820, with Mary and Dorothy, Mr. and Mrs. Monkhouse, and Crabb Robinson, he made a Continental tour lasting from July to November, their course being Brussels, Cologne, the Rhine, Switzerland, the Italian Lakes, Milan, returning by Paris, where they spent a month and all visited Annette and Caroline. Dorothy and Mary each kept journals, which served Wordsworth when, during the following year, he composed his *Memorials of a Tour* (published 1822). In the summer of 1823 he made a tour of Holland and Belgium. The following autumn he wandered all round North Wales with Mary and Dora, visiting his old friend Robert Jones, and the celebrated Ladies of Llangollen ; 1828 took him again to the Rhineland and Holland, this time with Dora and Coleridge. At Bonn " all the illuminati " of the place flocked to the house where they were staying. Schlegel was tactless enough to praise Byron. " Byron is a meteor," Coleridge cried out. " Wordsworth there is a ' star luminous and fixed.' " Unhappily the Germans have still not learned any better.

In the autumn of 1829 he visited Hamilton, the astronomer, in Ireland. In 1830 he rode all the way from Rydal to Cambridge to take Dora, who was staying with Christopher, now Master of Trinity, her pony. The next September he made his fourth tour of Scotland, and visited Scott at Abbotsford for the last time. The occasion brought forth several great poems, including *Yarrow Revisited* with its hardly bearable pathos –

> Past, present, future all appeared
>   In harmony united,
> Like guests that meet, and some from far,
>   By cordial love invited –

where they " clomb the winding stair " of Newark together, and, looking back to the river, knew that it would flow on for ever in the beauty of other poets long after they were gone. He also wrote his noble sonnet, " A trouble not of clouds," in farewell to Scott.

His last visit to Scotland was made in 1833, when he travelled with his son John and Crabb Robinson. They went by way of the Isle of Man in order to visit Mary's sailor-brother, Henry Hutchinson, the " retired mariner " ; and proceeded by Greenock to Oban, Staffa, and Iona, thence wandering back to the south.

In March 1837 – he was now sixty-seven years old – he crossed to the Continent for the last time. His companion was again Crabb Robinson, and Moxon, the publisher, was with them for part of the journey. They did not return to England till August, having made in the meantime an extensive tour of Italy, returning by Austria, Bavaria, and the Rhine. *The Memorials of a Tour in Italy* were the fruit of this journey, many of them being coloured with a political interest. At Rome they visited the graves of Keats and Shelley, and called on Joseph Severn.

Before he left home he had been harassed by proof-correcting for the fifth collected edition of his poems. From Salzburg he wrote a letter home which shows in a true light the sincerity of their domestic affections.

Dearest Mary, when I have felt how harshly I often demeaned myself to you, my inestimable fellow-labourer, while correcting the last edition of my poems, I often pray to God that he would grant us both life, that I may make some amends to you for that, and all my unworthiness. But you know into what an irritable state this overstrained labour often put my nerves. My impatience was ungovernable, as I *then* thought, but I now feel that it ought to have been governed. You have forgiven me, I know, as you did then; and perhaps that somehow troubles me the more. I say nothing of this to you, dear Dora, though you also have had some reason to complain.

For Mary, with the most penetrating instinct for what was required of her and the truest alliance of sense and sensibility that was ever found in poet's wife, served him and protected him, urged him to his poetry, and attended its labour through nearly fifty years of their lives. Writing his letters, copying his poems, nursing Dorothy, keeping the house, she served him with absolute devotion yet lost nothing of her own character, and gave him equally the wit and the criticism which was almost as useful as her love. And if, when they were first lovers, he had been strangely silent about her in his poetry, he made some amends later.

> True beauty dwells in deep retreats,
>   Whose veil is unremoved
> Till heart with heart in concord beats,
>   And the lover is beloved.

There are reasons for thinking that both William and Mary increased in physical beauty with age; and one and all the visitors to Rydal agreed in calling hers " the most beautiful old age we have ever seen."

The circle of Rydal is a fascinating picture, but a few names must suffice to suggest it – most of them disagreeing with the poet in particular opinions, none afraid to argue and criticise, but one and all acknowledging him as the greatest man of his age : Miss Jewsbury, the Arnolds at Fox How, Mrs. Fletcher, " the beautiful," of Llancrigg, Quillinan his son-in-law, the eccentric Miss Martineau, and, most useful of them all, Isabella Fenwick, to whom in his last years he dictated the notes on his poems which contain some of his best prose, and illuminating explanations of his philosophy.

His fame grew slowly, but when it came it overwhelmed him. For year after year not a day passed without the post bringing him manuscripts for criticism and requests for advice. Excursion trains were run to Windermere, and enthusiasts poured all over his garden. But other occasions warmed him with the frankness of their sincerity. When in 1839 the University of Oxford honoured him with a D.C.L. the ovation which greeted him was one of the most tremendous which the Sheldonian Theatre has ever witnessed. Admirers had travelled from all over the country " to join in the shout." In 1843, on Southey's death, he was offered the Laureateship, and at first declined the responsibility, but the wording of a second pressing request made further refusal impossible. The Lord Chamberlain assured him that it was " intended merely as an honorary distinction for the past, without the smallest reference to any service to be attached to it."

For that past had been not only the most significant of any poet then living, but one of the richest careers in the whole history of poetry. Ten years before his death he wrote to his American editor, Henry Reed : " I am standing on the brink of that vast ocean I must sail so soon – I must speedily lose sight of the shore and I could not once have conceived how little I am now troubled by the thought of how long or short a time they who remain on that shore may have sight of me. . . . It is well however, I am convinced," he added, " that men think otherwise in the earlier part of their lives " – as he himself had thought long years before, when he wrote in simple confidence to comfort Lady Beaumont's distress at the scorn in which his poems were then held.

" Trouble not yourself upon their present reception," he bade her ; " of what moment is that compared with what I trust is their destiny ? – to console the afflicted ; to add sunshine to daylight, by making the happy happier ; to teach the young and the gracious of every age to see, to think, and feel, and, therefore, to become more actively and securely virtuous ; this is their office, which I trust they will faithfully perform, long after we (that is, all that is mortal of us) are mouldered in our graves."

Wordsworth's hope was neither presumptuous nor vain. " What we have loved," he wrote, " others will love " ; and the words have been fulfilled.

In March 1850, a little before his eightieth birthday, he fell ill ; and upon St. George's Day, doubly remembered in the coming and going of Shakespeare, Wordsworth died. Four days later, the earth, whose prophet he had been, took back in the churchyard at Grasmere the body which had held one of the greatest spirits of all time.

BIBLIOGRAPHY

The Poems of William Wordsworth, edited by Nowell C. Smith. Three Volumes. Methuen 1908. The best working edition.

The Oxford Wordsworth, and Macmillan's Wordsworth (which is arranged as far as possible in chronological order) are convenient for general purposes.

The Prelude, edited from the manuscripts by Ernest de Selincourt. Oxford 1926. (Cheap reprint of the 1805 text 1933.)

The Prose Works of William Wordsworth, edited by Alexander Grosart. Three volumes. Moxon 1876. (Out of print.)

Literary Criticism, ed. Nowell Smith.

Tract on the Convention of Cintra, ed. Dicey.

Guide to the Lakes, ed. E. de Selincourt.

The last three are obtainable in *The Oxford Miscellany*.

The Early Letters of William and Dorothy Wordsworth, edited by E. de Selincourt. Oxford 1935. (To be followed by further volumes.)

Correspondence of Crabb Robinson with the Wordsworth Circle, edited by Edith J. Morley. Two volumes. Oxford 1927.

Wordsworth and Reed, edited by L. N. Broughton. Oxford 1933.

Journals of Dorothy Wordsworth, edited by William Knight. Macmillan.

Unfortunately only a somewhat arbitrary selection. But further extracts may be found in :—

Dorothy Wordsworth, by Ernest de Selincourt, Oxford 1933, from which the facts of Wordsworth's own life may be more accurately obtained than anywhere else.

Critical biographies and studies include :

William Wordsworth, by G. M. Harper.   Murray.

The Early Life of William Wordsworth, by E. Legouis.
    Dent.   (Supplemented by *William Wordsworth
    and Annette Vallon* by Legouis, Dent.)

The Later Wordsworth, by E. C. Batho.   Cambridge.

Wordsworth, by Walter Raleigh.   Arnold.

Wordsworth, by H. W. Garrod ; and " Wordsworth's
    Lucy " in the same author's *Profession of
    Poetry*. Both Oxford.

Wordsworth, by C. H. Herford.   Routledge.

Wordsworth, by F. W. H. Myers.   *English Men of
    Letters*.   1881.

"Mr. Burra is to be congratulated on the adroitness with which he has succeeded in including in this book all that is essential to a knowledge of the man and the poet . . . There can be no two opinions over the quality of Mr. Burra's appreciation of the poetry itself."—*Spectator*.

This edition, specially issued for the Wordsworth Centenary in 1950, includes a portrait frontispiece reproduced by kind permission of Mrs. Rawnsley.